INTANGIBLE: Yasushi Tanaka and Louise G. Cann, A Marriage of Artist and Author

Denise Tanaka

Published by Sasoriza Books, 2022.

INTANGIBLE: YASUSHI TANAKA AND LOUISE G. CANN, A MARRIAGE OF ARTIST AND AUTHOR

First edition. January 9, 2022.

ISBN: 978-1946055071

Written by Denise Tanaka.

to my husband Hiroshi

Intangible

INTANGIBLE
Yasushi Tanaka and Louise G. Cann
A Marriage of Artist and Author

by Denise B. Tanaka

Published by Sasoriza Books

Sasoriza Books

www.sasorizabooks.com

https://www.facebook.com/SasorizaBooks

Cover art by Elina Tanaka

Dedicated to my husband Hiroshi

Prologue

I stumbled onto the romance of artist Yasushi Tanaka and poet Louise G. Cann while researching another project. Scrolling through historical newspapers from 1917, my own married name popped off the page. Tanaka is in the top five most common surnames in Japan so there is no relation. Even so, the words of Miss Cann aroused my curiosity and fascination.

Once upon a time, I too was a red-headed American girl who left home for college. I met a foreign student from Japan, got married, and made a life together. If we had lived a hundred years ago, our experience would have been very different.

Louise Cann found her soul mate in Seattle, Washington but the restrictive immigration laws of the late 19th century prohibited marriage of inter-racial couples. They appeared before a local judge to plead for a waiver and be issued a marriage license. Louise argued her case in court, and to society at large, that she felt attracted to Tanaka for his artistic and philosophical mind. She eloquently made the case that their souls had connected on a cosmic level. As a poet and an artist, they shared an intangible, esoteric view of the world. They assured the judge of their commitment to a stable marriage and their expectations of a happy life. She won the judge's approval and officially became Mrs. Yasushi Tanaka.

The Tanakas strived to create a progressive style of marriage that shed the stifling trappings of Victorian-era conventions. Their marriage was unique for those days in that she did not play the role of subservient housewife and he did not discourage her from a career as an author and a scholar. Throughout the decades, she continued to use her maiden name on her published works of art critiques and biographies. Within social circles, she could happily be Mrs. Tanaka but her professional byline would continue to be Miss Cann. The Tanakas shared a partnership as creative, intellectual equals and fully supported each other in their professional endeavors.

I dug into their life stories in search of what circumstances brought them together and what indefinable qualities sustained them through the hardships they endured in the first half of the 20th century. External forces threatened to tear them apart, but through all of it, Louise stayed constant and true to Yasushi. Without her support early in his art career, he never would have thrived to the extent that he did. Without her curatorship, his paintings would have been lost to the dustbin of history. Here is the untold story of an artist who has been too long overlooked.

Table of Contents

PART I
Seattle

In my search for understanding the mind and heart of this extraordinary woman, I found it necessary to explore Louise Cann's personal origins. Her family background informs how she developed a fierce sense of independence. What were the circumstances of her childhood? Who disapproved of her choice to marry someone from the other side of the world? What did she gain or lose by rebelling against the conservative norms of early 20th century America?

Louise Cann's Father

THOMAS HART CANN, BORN circa 1833 in Illinois, lost his father when he was 15 years old. At the age of 20, he left home to tag along with a wagon train to seek his fortune in the gold mines of California. He journeyed over sands and mountains, forged rivers and crossed deserts to reach what he called "the land of sunshine and plenty" in a place called Hang Town—now Placerville, California. At six feet in height, and barely over a hundred pounds, his companions called him a beanpole. On his first Sunday morning after arriving in town, he ventured into a nearby church and tried to be inconspicuous sitting in the back. The clergyman noticed him, pulled him out into the open, and welcomed him with a loud cry of "Glory to God!" Although he felt embarrassed with his tattered garments, worn-out shoes and sunburned face, he thrilled at the acceptance of the congregation. Years later, he fondly reminisced on the many friends he made that day.

Typical of so many Gold Rush prospectors who rushed westward with dreams shining in their eyes, he never got rich by dipping a pan in a creek to find a sparkle in the mud. He turned to a series of steady but more dangerous jobs as a deputy sheriff in Idaho, or as a parcel deliveryman for Wells, Fargo & Co. riding horseback through bitter snows and outlaw territory or aboard steamboats on the Snake and Columbia rivers.

He served as a land commissioner in Oregon for eight years, during which time he began a law practice. Thomas Cann relocated north to Seattle, Washington where he practiced law, served as a police judge, and was a justice of the peace. Politically, he supported the Republican Party as it was in the 19th century, the party of Davy Crockett and Abraham Lincoln. He proudly cast his first presidential vote in 1856 for John C. Fremont.

His biography, published in a local history book, included a generous testimonial of one of his peers, a fellow judge. "I consider him one of the most active, thorough and successful members of the profession. During his term of service on the bench here he made himself a terror to the evildoers, and did much to improve the moral tone of the community. He had to a remarkable degree that rare ability for detecting truth from falsehood, for unearthing fraud and hypocrisy, which is so necessary in a committing magistrate. In his practice he has received a large clientage, and is entrusted with many important interests. He has the unbounded confidence of his clients and is, I believe, in the enjoyment of as remunerative a practice as any lawyer in Seattle."

Thomas Hart Cann married in 1864 in Portland, Oregon to eighteen-year-old Louisa Anne Gephart (alt. Gebhard), a native of Hamburg, Germany who had immigrated to America. Her parents were from Germany and France, respectively, which in those days was something of a mixed marriage. More dedicated researchers than I may someday uncover the reasons for Louisa Gephart leaving Europe after the turmoil of the Napoleonic Wars, if she came alone or with a family group, or how she arrived in Oregon in the 1860s. I know that by living in the Pacific Northwest with her new American husband, Louisa Gephart avoided the bloody Franco-Prussian War of 1870 that disrupted the European balance of power for decades to come.

The newly-married Canns settled in a riverside town called The Dalles, Oregon that marked the end point of the Oregon Trail. The 1880 federal census shows Thomas Cann living in a comfortable home with his wife and three small children: Adaline at age 15, Thomas Hart Cann Jr. at age 13, and—with a significant gap—the infant Louise. I have no information on whether more children were lost in between, but such a large age gap surely contributed to Louise's sense of separateness and isolation. By the time Louise started her first day of school, her sister was a grown woman of twenty and her brother was a capable man of eighteen.

Their household in 1880 also includes a Chinese servant age 26 known in the census record only as Chung. Judge Cann regularly employed servants who came from Asia and who, in contrast to his wife, could never legally immigrate under the restrictive laws of the time. Beginning in the late 1840s and 1850s, thousands of Chinese crossed the Pacific Ocean to flee poverty or civil upheavals in their own country. Yet they were discouraged from digging for gold, by laws such as the Foreign Miners Tax and by outright violence. They turned to roles of domestic service or hard labor. Chinese immigrants built much of the infrastructure in the western United States—the railroad tracks and tunnels through the Sierra Nevada mountains—and yet laws prohibited them from owning property or from marrying whomever they wished.

Louise grew up in a multi-lingual household, with her mother likely speaking French and the servants speaking Chinese. The Asians that her father viewed as "others" were familiar companions to Louise at home. Then, the family relocated and gave her a taste of the pioneering wanderlust as a small child. They settled in the growing boom town of Seattle, Washington. This major seaport of the west coast was a jumping off point to Alaska's Klondike territory—the second big gold rush after California—and a major gateway to immigrants from the Far East. So, from her earliest days of childhood, Louise was exposed to a cosmopolitan atmosphere. She could gaze out at the horizon of the great Pacific Ocean and imagine a larger world beyond.

Louise Cann's Brother

THOMAS HART CANN, JR., like his namesake father, studied law and passed the bar exam. He began his law career working as a bailiff of the district court. He also helped to organize a local militia group called the Seattle Rifles and advanced to the rank of sergeant. This militia group, Company D, was involved with maintaining civil order during Seattle's infamous Chinatown riot.

Anti-Chinese sentiment was at a fever pitch in the 1880s with the passage of federal laws such as the Chinese Exclusion Act of 1882 that restricted un-skilled Asian laborers from coming to the U.S. Once their cheap labor had been exploited to build railroads, bridges, and tunnels through the mountains, the Asian immigrants on the west coast turned into a bogeyman that white citizens called a threat. Louise's father, Judge Cann, wrote an opinion editorial saying, "We would be better off without Chinese," around the time of the race riots in the city.

Seattle's Chinese Riot of 1886 occurred as the climax to a number of smaller outbreaks of violence in the streets. White residents for months had been harassing the Chinese immigrants who worked as servants or manual laborers in town. On February 7, 1886 an armed mob, with the full cooperation of Seattle police, stormed into the Chinatown district. They went house-to-house and hauled over three hundred people out of their homes or businesses. They marched them to the city's wharf where the rioters had chartered a steamship to transport them away.

Thomas Cann Jr., at just eighteen years old, joined Sheriff McGraw and The Seattle Rifles to intervene against the rioting mob. Confrontations in the streets resulted in several injuries and one man's death. The governor of Washington declared martial law and called for assistance from federal troops who stayed through the summer to patrol the streets.

A majority of the Chinese residents chose to leave Seattle, anyway, rather than stay in such a hostile environment. They traveled south to California and joined the communities of Chinese in Los Angeles or San Francisco. Only a handful stayed behind in Seattle for a slow, painful recovery; it would take decades for Seattle's Chinatown to return to its pre-1885 population levels. Immigrants from other Asian countries, most notably Japan, arrived to fill the void in Seattle's International District. Once again, the white citizens were anything but welcoming. Federal laws prohibited Asians of any nationality from ever naturalizing as citizens. The Washington state constitution barred Asians from owning real estate—not the soil of the farms they worked and not the land underneath their businesses in town.

Perhaps the ugliness that he witnessed in his fellow citizens changed Thomas Cann Jr.'s perspective on continuing a career in law enforcement. After the 1886 riot, he changed course and chose the open sea. He abandoned his future as a lawyer and turned to a seafarer's life on the merchant ships. Thomas went north to Alaska to work for the Pacific Coast Steamship Company and rarely set foot on dry land again. Aboard cargo ships, he found a new purpose in transporting freight and passengers up and down the coast between the Gulf of Alaska, the Pacific Northwest, and the San Francisco Bay. In 1903, in his mid-thirties, he became a captain. Throughout his career, he commanded over twenty different steamships. He married a local Seattle girl named Edna True, a woman who must have spent many hours gazing out the window for her husband's ship to pull into port.

Thomas Cann Jr.'s character is revealed in how he conducted himself in a tragic incident—a shipwreck that occurred just a year after the famed *Titanic* went down in an eerily similar manner. To this day, Captain Thomas Cann's steamship the SS *State of California* lies under two hundred feet of chilly dark waters off the coast of Alaska.

On that fateful morning of August 17, 1913, the waters at Gambier Bay were calm under clear summer skies. The crew and 55 passengers had enjoyed breakfast while the ship unloaded cargo to the wharf. So far, everything looked routine. Captain Cann and his chief pilot were experienced seafarers familiar with the nautical charts and maps. They remained vigilant as they chugged away from shore and fired up the boilers, full-steam-ahead, on course to the middle of the channel.

The ship's hull struck a submerged rock where the maps wrongly showed safe passage. Captain Cann later testified, "She kept going. It was not a solid impact; she went right over it." The rocky reef sliced open the hull's bottom as a chef's knife would gut a fish. The whole ship rolled hard from one side to the other as water rushed inside.

Captain Cann instantly realized that the ship would go to the bottom of the bay in a matter of minutes. He sounded the alarm and ordered his crew to help passengers onto lifeboats. He steered toward a sandbank and tried to run aground. The flooded engines stopped turning and he had no more forward thrust. The ship quickly slipped backwards into deeper water. A few lifeboats had managed to carry survivors but had no time to row away from the churning waters of the sinking ship. A falling steam stack crushed one lifeboat. Another lifeboat became tangled in floating lines and got dragged underwater.

Still on the bridge, Captain Cann held his station as the sinking ship crumbled all around him. Just three minutes after striking the rock, the pilothouse and chart room broke apart. Captain Cann and his pilot plunged into freezing water. The pilothouse bobbed to the surface and stayed afloat well enough for the captain to climb onto it. While straddling the sinking wreckage, he shouted orders to his crew in lifeboats to row back into the chaos and pull survivors from the water.

Rescue boats from the wharf reached the scene within minutes, just in time to watch the steamship disappear beneath the water. Working together with the few lifeboats that remained afloat, they scooped up the men and women clinging to broken debris. In all, 31 lives were lost. Roughly half of those aboard survived.

Two separate inquiries held in Juneau, Alaska and in Seattle, Washington absolved Captain Cann of any wrongdoing. The crew and passengers unanimously praised his swift, decisive actions for saving as many people as he did. Errors in the nautical charts were amended to mark the newly found obstruction. Afterwards, he would say, "When a chart is incorrect, it is much much worse than none at all." He deeply felt the loss of life and always wished he could have done more.

Ironically, her brother's life would come to an end a decade later, on land, in the act of helping someone. On the evening of Sunday, March 8, 1925, a neighbor was having trouble with his automobile. Thomas Cann went into the road to help push the disabled vehicle off to the side for safety. At the worst possible moment, another driver came speeding around the bend and did not have time to stomp the brakes. He struck Captain Cann who died at the scene. He was 57 years old.

Louise Cann's Sister

ADALINE CANN, THE OLDEST of the three siblings, never married and never left her parents' home to live on her own. By the customs of the day, she would be called a spinster—a term commonly applied to unmarried women. Her life appears to be the opposite of her younger sister in that she avoided the limelight and did not challenge the status quo.

It's unfortunate that in the strict patriarchal society of the early 20th century, attention was given only to the men of the family. Local history books published biographies of Seattle's prominent citizens of the day, but only the men are showcased. These books were common in the late 19th and early 20th century, written by interviews and with considerable input from the subjects. Judge Cann's biography highlights the accomplishments of his male ancestors and of himself. His son Captain Cann likewise in his autobiographic profile gives a resume of his maritime career. Typical of the style of the day, women are mentioned only briefly as accessories. If a wife's family background did not include prestigious figures, then even their maiden names are inconsequential.

Through exhaustive research into local newspaper archives, I have only managed to find snippets of Adaline Cann in Seattle's local society pages. She participated in women's art and literature clubs meeting with tea and cookies at each other's homes. She is on the membership committee for the Clionian Club dedicated to the study of classical, noncontroversial literature. She read presentations on such topics as the practical study of stained glass for the West Seattle Art Club. Her obituary notes that she had a prominent, active role in the St. John's Episcopal Church community.

Washington state enacted laws granting women the right to vote in 1910, joining other states in a growing national campaign that culminated in passage of the 19th Amendment to the U.S. Constitution in 1920. Although she may not have joined the ranks of Susan B. Anthony and suffragettes marching in the streets for the right to vote, once the ink dried on the 19th amendment, Adeline Cann dutifully worked the polls as an election official.

In contrast to her sister Louise, it appears that Adaline conformed to society's expectations for a proper, post-Victorian woman. She pursued an appreciation of arts and literature of the socially acceptable kind. Adeline embodies all of the small-minded, provincial, Victorian, rigid conventions that Louise herself fought to escape. It appears that Louise—with her radical modernistic ideas—became estranged from her parents and her older sister.

Louise Cann's Ex-Husband

EVEN BEFORE SHE MET her cosmic soul mate Yasushi Tanaka, Louise and her family were at odds. Not that she didn't try to fit the mold of society's expectations at first. Before she married her soul mate Yasushi Tanaka, Louise Cann married and divorced the type of man that her parents whole-heartedly approved. Her unhappiness in her first marriage was compounded by her restless independent soul under the strain of conforming to her family's and society's expectations.

Arthur Ranum was a professor of mathematics on faculty at the University of Washington, in Seattle. A man nearly 10 years older than Louise, he was born in Wisconsin to parents who had immigrated from Norway. Louise and Arthur were married on October 5, 1899 in St. Martin's Church in Seattle, with her sister Adaline the bridesmaid standing happily by her side. Louise wore a lovely gown described in the newspapers and her future seemed bright.

Honeymoon bliss quickly faded. Louise was desperately unhappy in this marriage, based on what she said later in interviews and in the recurring themes of her published fiction. Her short story "Annette" is a tale of a woman who marries a grieving widower, emotionally distant and pining over his late wife; in the end, the widower comes to the epiphany that his grief has caused him to neglect his current wife.

Arthur Ranum's obituary written by the faculty of Cornell University gives a glimpse into the man's character. "His writings are remarkable for their style and elegance. The subject matter is presented as a complete and harmonious whole; the procedure is strikingly simple and direct; laborious proofs are avoided; and the reader is left with an impression of the richness and beauty of the total conception. The effect is due partly to Professor Ranum's care in thinking through his subject, and partly to his rare genius for presentation. These talents and his accurate scholarship made him an able teacher. He had a remarkable gift for making the most recondite ideas understandable and attractive."

On the other hand, the obituary also reveals that his personality was "quiet and self-effacing. He had a considerable element of stoicism in his nature." At first, no doubt Louise Cann admired his intelligence and his disciplined writing craft although she had no interest in abstract theories of geometry or algebra. His emotional detachment is likely what drove her away.

Louise played the dutiful wife for about fifteen years. She and Arthur never had children, whether by choice or by physical inability is impossible to ever know. She uprooted her own life and traveled with him coast-to-coast, wherever her husband wished to pursue his academic career. Yet while Arthur Ranum faced no obstacles in accomplishing his goals, Louise struggled to gain a foothold as a journalist and an author.

Arthur Ranum left his faculty post at the University of Washington and, from 1904 to 1905, he taught mathematics at the University of Wisconsin. The following year, he taught at Stanford University in Palo Alto, California. Arthur earned his Ph.D. in Mathematics in 1906 from the University of Chicago with a dissertation titled, "The Group of Classes of Congruent Matrices with Application to the Group of Isomorphisms of Any Abelian Group." His next stop was to earn a place as an instructor at Cornell University in Ithaca, New York where he would remain on faculty for the rest of his life. He worked his way up the ranks for about a decade before he earned tenure as a professor.

While living briefly in California, Louise continued the journalism career that she had started in Seattle by doing women's calendar events for the local newspaper. She wrote a book review column for the *San Francisco Call* newspaper under her married name Louise Ranum. But her true passion was for cutting-edge modern literature, fiction and poetry. In 1910, she published "Dreams" a collection of her poems through the Poet Lore Company. Her style is still somewhat amateurish, an imitation of Longfellow at times, but with the consistent theme of a restless soul struggling to break free. Her poems have such titles as, The Quest, The Woman Misunderstood, The Wordless Soul, Yearning, Melancholy, Inconstancy, and Oh - The Thrill of Life.

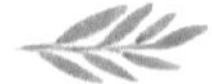

INCONSTANCY

Not more restless than my heart
Is the restless sea;
Not more vagrant than my heart

Is the great wind's vagrancy.
Fleeting as the opal sheen
Sunrise spills on ocean's green
Are the fleet moods of my heart.
Fluid is this world of change,
Fluid are the thoughts that range
To seize on meanings of the change;
Fluid as the torrent stream
That hastes to die in ocean's dream
Is emotion in my heart.

—Louise Gebhard Cann (as Louise Ranum)
"Dreams" 1910

SHE TOOK CLASSES AT Cornell in the class of 1909. While studying in the humanities department, she discovered exciting new ideas of the modernists and socialists and all the other "-ists" of the early 20th century. While her husband devoted himself to theories of mathematics, Louise eagerly devoured the writings of James Joyce, T.S. Eliot, and Ezra Pound. She published another volume of poetry, now out of print and lost for all time.

Her one-act play, never performed on stage, is titled, "Life is Always the Same." It was published years later, in 1919, in a quarterly journal, *The Drama*, but my hunch is that she wrote it much earlier. The main character is described as "...a large, swarthy woman, of about thirty-five, whose figure has been distorted by corset-wearing... stands at the windows gazing out moodily." On a stormy night, a bearded traveler asks for shelter. Twenty pages of dialogue brings the woman to the realization that this disheveled vagabond is actually her husband! Not only was he presumed dead, but she had hired someone to throw him off a cliff. He survived with enough disfigurements to his face and voice that she did not recognize him. Her accomplice was caught, confessed to murder, and executed on the gallows. Oh, and guess who was the hangman?

The presumed-dead husband's final act of revenge was to reassert dominance over her life. He says, "You'll know how it feels to have a dead man for a master..." These are the play's final lines with grim undertones hinting at a violent, tragic resolution:

SHE (*succumbing to the fact that his hand is on her*): You want to be my master? (*shrilly*) Well, be it! But since, after all, you're alive, I'll give you something to do. Yes! (*She nods her head fiercely.*) I'll give you something to do, hangman. (*She stands looking at him with malign stubbornness.*)

HE (*with satire*): Life is always the same, eh?

Louise did not finish her baccalaureate degree because of what she later described as "financial hardship." In other words, even though her husband was on the faculty at Cornell University, Arthur Ranum did not support his wife earning a degree of her own. My speculation is that a man steeped in the world of mathematics could not appreciate the value of the arts and humanities. If she had pursued more conservative studies, would he have supported her? Or perhaps he wished for Louise to give up her own career to be a housewife and produce children—something that she was either unable or unwilling to do.

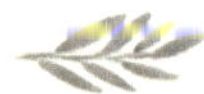

Louise Cann, Divorcée

LOUISE QUIT COLLEGE and left her husband for New York City. She arrived alone with no money, no friends, and no prospects of employment. She applied to the Sun newspaper and became a regular literary contributor for about two years. This shows her independent spirit as women journalists were a rare commodity in the early teen years of the 20th century. Women generally wrote fluff pieces for the society or gossip columns. Louise sought alternative assignments to interview artists or authors in the New York art and literary scene. She wrote book reviews with a strong slant of literary analysis.

After a few years working for the newspaper in New York City, Louise returned to Seattle with intent to write a novel, but more importantly, to finally end her unhappy marriage. The reason she did not file for divorce in New York is obvious. At the time, New York's laws only allowed one reason for divorce—adultery—whereas the state of Washington offered more legal options. She could not afford lawyers or a court battle, and she had no grounds to accuse Arthur Ranum of adultery.

Louise filed for divorce in Washington superior court on September 29, 1913 for reasons of nonsupport as reported in the legal announcements of the *Seattle Daily Times* the following day. Clearly, Arthur Ranum took no action to fight it. The decree of divorce was granted a few weeks later. She officially dropped her married name of Ranum and resumed using her maiden name Louise Cann.

In all likelihood, her parents and older sister shunned her for abandoning Arthur Ranum. I imagine they counseled her to make amends with her ex-husband, to apologize and beg to be remarried. Louisa's willful independence caused a rift that would never be repaired. Victorian Era traditions of a woman's role as submissive wife and mother were being challenged by Louise's generation. In a short autobiography that she wrote years later, for being profiled in a newspaper, Louise proclaimed, "that the time is coming when all marriages will be simply a matter of registration; when wedding rings will disappear; when women will not change their names, but keep their own, and will be addressed as 'Miss,' whether married or single, and when children will be designated by the mother's surname."

She leveraged her experience in New York City to gain a position on the local Seattle newspaper, still writing book reviews or interviews of local artists. At this point in her life, she reinvented herself and set new goals for her literary career. Louise dared to be a divorcée at a time when it was scandalous in polite society; women often lied about being widowed rather than admit to a failed marriage. By then, Seattle was becoming a hub for a growing fine arts community. In addition to the small-minded, conservative society ladies holding tea parties, another group was rising to prominence: the Seattle Fine Arts Society.

Louise Meets Yasushi

LOUISE FIRST ENCOUNTERED Yasushi Tanaka as a well-established artist in the local Seattle community. She knew nothing of his background, how he had left behind his widowed mother and half a dozen siblings to come to America alone. As a youth of eighteen years old, Yasushi had arrived in

Seattle, Washington without a clear plan for the future other than to express his creative mind. In the decade in between his arrival and meeting Louise, he had studied with local artists to develop his skills in European-style oil painting to the point of establishing himself as a rising talent in the local art scene. He had already exhibited at one-man shows and taught art students in studio and outdoor classes.

When he gave a public lecture at the Seattle Fine Arts Association in September 1914, she sat quietly in the audience. The *Seattle Sunday Times* advertised the event with a glowing endorsement. "Yasushi Tanaka, a Japanese artist of ability who has won fame and distinction for his futurist work, will give a lecture on futurist and cubist art work."

At the lecture, Louise felt thrilled to hear Yasushi discuss esoteric ideas that she shared with university colleagues in New York but no one in provincial Seattle understood. Whatever he said in that lecture is lost to time, however, Yasushi published an opinion piece soon afterwards, titled "Art As It Should Be," in *The Town Crier*—a weekly arts and culture magazine. This piece gives an early, unfiltered view of Yasushi's perspective on art in relation to early 20th century philosophy. "Art in its spontaneous sense, is decidedly a spiritual matter itself, rather than its limitless possibilities being diffused in its scope of ever-developing human consciousness and intelligence about it. To study art, then, is precisely to deal with something of spiritual significance. By spiritual significance we mean the vital and condensed reason of underlying natural forces or motives, which complete both mental and material revelations in various forms.... Art is strictly an individual matter; that is, the manifestation of the individual mental and spiritual activities. It never could nor should be formulated. It is not the mere expected result itself with some certain prescribed method for the means but the very reason of the doing itself that stands indispensable for the individual need of expression. And the truth of it always lies in its fundamental conception of graphic and plastic expression, the theory of which has an extremely philosophic importance, and needs a considerable meta-physical investigation and psychological research."

Louise was instantly dazzled by his modernistic ideas of viewing the new modalities of art through the lens of modern philosophy. How amazed she felt to hear a man born in a country so far away speak the same ideas that she had been exposed to in college, and thoughts that she had dreamed within herself.

"He expressed the very opinions which I have been laughed at for having," she says, "and I desired to explore his wonderful mind."

The Seattle Fine Arts Association was home base for a number of local artists who would later gain national recognition. One founding member, the renowned photographer Imogen Cunningham, was a free-spirited soul who rejected the Victorian ideas that a woman's role in life should be defined only by the 3 Ks: *Kinder, Küche, Kirche*, a German slogan translated as children, kitchen, church. She studied at the University of Washington but when it did not offer photography classes, she earned a degree in chemistry with a focus on the scientific processes of photography. She experimented with techniques for developing film and stands among the luminaries of early photography. She took her first artistic photographs on the university campus—a self-portrait of herself lying nude in the grass. This photo is remarkable in that it is not erotic and it does not mimic classical Greek or Renaissance themes; it is simply a woman in her natural state reclining in the grass. She snapped a series of nude portraits of the man who would become her husband, Roy Partridge, against a background of natural scenery. She published her photographs in art journals and paid the bills by taking studio portraits of local citizens.

Two of Imogen Cunningham's early photographs are relevant here. One is a portrait of an anonymous Japanese model, titled "Boy With Incense" reproduced in *Wilson's Photography Magazine* in 1914 but likely taken a year or two earlier. The resemblance is strikingly similar to the only known photograph of Yasushi's lifelong friend Ichizo "Issio" Kuge.

The other is a portrait photograph of Yasushi Tanaka himself, in a rare pose of almost feminine vulnerability, dressed in a light-colored kimono similar to the one worn by "Boy With Incense." A small ikebana-type flower arrangement is used as an accent prop. The date of this photograph is approximate, as Cunningham was notorious for not labeling her works.

Most likely, Yasushi and his friend worked as handyman laborers on the farm of Imogen Cunningham's pioneer father. One can easily imagine that, when Isaac Cunningham famously converted a shed on his property into a photographic darkroom for his daughter, he employed Japanese laborers to do the work. Yasushi saw himself as more than a hired laborer, and perhaps had ambitions of a more intimate relationship with Ms. Cunningham. He wrote her personal letters—of which only a few survive—that range from a cordial report on a road trip to California to an emotionally-charged, rambling apology penned in April 1913. "There can be no fixed and definite formula for living a life. Human life? That's nothing but a bit of truthful nature upon human flesh, and that's all. But Time is passing! Alas! My dear friend, this very thought or idea is constantly and incessantly driving me forth; I have to get rid of it, and I have to rule it by my own effort.... I paint for my life's sake; I don't paint because I live; but I paint in order that I may live. And I want to paint more because I want to live more - not necessarily longer, of course. Pity me, good friend, I may be of insane insanity. I am always desiring to know my friends better—if necessary—and I have to know you better because it is of absolute necessity. So I have explained myself for the same reason and I believe you know me better now. And I, truly and sincerely, remain your most worth-while-knowing friend."

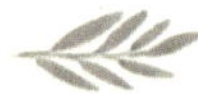

Yasushi Tanaka's Background

YASUSHI TANAKA EXPERIENCED a unique period of Japanese history that both shaped and nurtured his creative spirit. He is the first one in his family to leave his homeland, and if not for a series of geopolitical events, he might never have come to the United States or met Louise Cann, his soulmate. One wonders, what circumstances brought Yasushi Tanaka to Seattle and what drove his ambitions to stand apart from his fellow countrymen, to pursue artistic expression on canvas as illustrations of his philosophical views?

The Empire of Japan in Yasushi's lifetime was a drastically different landscape from what his own father knew, and in turn was radically different from his own grandfather's life experience. In the space of roughly forty years, Japan ended its draconian policy of isolation and in the 1870s opened up to the world. Overnight, the country transformed from medieval feudalism to an open-borders industrial nation. The samurai class was abolished. The lowly peasants were allowed to have surnames. The country scrambled to transform from agriculture to 19th century technology with telephones, factories, gas lights, electricity, and railroads by the turn of the century. Scientists and intellectuals were imported from Europe to offer their knowledge as well as to gain insight into the mysterious land that had been locked away for over two centuries. The popular phrase of the era was to "catch up" with the West.

In fact, the government of Emperor Meiji was so eager to discard the dusty past and embrace European culture as the future that they undertook a program called *Haibutsu-Kisyaku* of destroying their own Buddhist statues and images. They closed a number of temples and forced Buddhist priests to renounce their vows for civilian occupations. As a result, Japan lost a huge number of cultural artifacts. Ironically, it was foreign residents who campaigned for preserving the traditional arts of Japan, such as the renowned scholar Ernest F. Fenollosa who taught political economy and philosophy at Tokyo Imperial University—a long-standing institution not far from Yasushi's home neighborhood.

Although the samurai class was officially abolished, those who had held prestige in society did not fully abandon their awareness of heritage. Somewhat comparable to the aristocratic gentlemen of the southern U.S. after the Civil War, everyone still knew who used to be who. The higher-ranking samurai rebranded themselves as aristocracy, taking on titles as dukes and barons. Emperor Meiji dressed in military jackets with gold braid on the shoulder and medals on his chest in the same style as European kings or the Tsar of Russia.

Yasushi Tanaka's family was of the samurai class but a bit lower on the ladder of hierarchy. His father had been in an administrative role under the samurai Lord Ooka until 1871 when all feudal domains were abolished and old allegiances were dissolved. In the new era of Emperor Meiji, his father served in a banking or finance capacity.

Yasushi Tanaka was born in 1886 (or, year 19 of the Meiji Imperial Era) in a town known as Ota-cho, today Iwasaki City, in the Saitama prefecture west of the capital city Tokyo. As the fourth son of nine children, he was essentially a middle child.

As mentioned earlier, Tanaka is an extremely common surname that translates to "middle-of-the-rice-field." Yasushi's first name shows a touch of creativity on his parents' part, a single *kanji* character that means preservation or to retaining an object for a long time. This same kanji can be alternately used for the names Tamotsu or Mamoru due to the flexibility of the writing system. Many of the original-language reference materials include phonetic script as a guide to the proper reading of his first name. Japan imported written characters from China over a thousand years ago and adapted the abstract pictorial characters to its own unique language. Today, in Japan, the *kanji* can be read aloud any number of ways depending on the context, either by retaining the original Chinese pronunciation or assigning a native Japanese word in combination with phonetic syllables. Personal names are notorious for variety and complexity to the point that, when meeting a new acquaintance, one of the first questions to ask is, "How do you write your name?"

Although rice fields surround the city to this day, Yasushi's upbringing was a vibrant, cosmopolitan environment. Men discarded their kimono for tailored suits and bowler hats. Foreign works of literature, in translation, flew hot off the presses alongside modern novels by Japanese authors. Yasushi attended school in Tokyo where he was exposed to exciting ideas from the outside, the paintings of European artists and the literature of other lands. Fine art schools were well established by the turn of the century, as foreigners had been pouring in through the Yokohama port for a few decades. European scholars like Professor Fenollosa were employed as teachers in public schools and private tutors to the wealthy citizens. Yasushi clearly studied the English language in school before he ever imagined traveling to America.

His father died in 1902 when Yasushi was sixteen years old. His older brothers worked to support their widowed mother as the family fell into hardship. The younger siblings, Yasushi included, continued to attend public school. Yasushi being lower on the list of siblings did not have the same obligations of filial responsibility as his oldest brother, the first-born son. This allowed him a bit more freedom to pursue his own creative interests.

By the time Yasushi graduated Urawa High School in 1904, Japan was embroiled in a major international war with Imperial Russia. Many young men like Yasushi were conscripted into the military. The Russo-Japanese War had erupted in February 1904 over the rival ambitions of each empire to expand their sphere of influence in Manchuria and the Korean peninsula. Catch up with the West? Japan certainly did. After two centuries of self-imposed isolation, Japan burst out of its borders to wage war with modern armaments and steam ships. The forces of Russia's Tsar Nicholas II suffered devastating and surprising defeats in a series of naval battles where the Japanese proved their skills in military strategy.

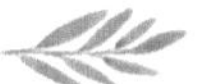

Yasushi Comes to America

YASUSHI LEFT JAPAN at the height of the Russo-Japanese war, perhaps to evade military service, and partly out of eagerness to discover a new world beyond the borders of the island nation. He saw fresh opportunities to explore new horizons that men of his grandfather's generation never had a chance to do.

At age eighteen, a few days before Christmas, December 21, 1904, Yasushi boarded the steamship *Kanagawa Maru* departing from Yokohama Harbor. The ship carried him across the wintery Pacific Ocean, around the curved coastline of the Alaska-Yukon Territory, down the shoreline of western Canada and the Puget Sound.

On January 9, 1905, he arrived in the port city of Seattle, Washington. The immigration record of arrival notes that he was a student, he carried $59 in his pocket, and the cost of his passage was paid by his older brother.

Did he come to America with the preconceived intent to study fine art? Or, did he come in search of opportunity and, by chance, stumbled into the study of art? Whatever thoughts filled the young man's mind, as he stepped off the steamship on that cold January day, will forever be a mystery.

Not much is known of Yasushi's early days living in Seattle's International District. He later described living hand to mouth, doing a variety of menial odd jobs such as a dishwasher, a peanut vendor, a cook, a fruit dealer, and a farm-worker. Once he sold a portrait for the price of a noodle bowl.

It is nearly impossible to trace Yasushi's activities in the early years because of the transient, vagabond lifestyle imposed on Asian immigrants by the racial bias of the society. Laws prohibited Asians from owning real estate property, which meant they could rent apartments but never own the apartment building. They could run shops or restaurants but could never own the land underneath the business. The inhabitants of Seattle's International District in the early 20th century lived under the shadow of the Chinese riots from twenty years earlier; who knew if, at any moment, another angry mob could erupt, drag them into the streets, and force them onto the next steamship out of town.

The Japanese who came from different regions in their home country, who spoke with different accents in a variety of dialects, nevertheless bonded together in the United States. In *espirit de corps,* the bonds formed of fellow persecuted strangers in a strange land. Immigrants sheltered and helped each other through formal organizations like the Buddhist temple or informally by long-time residents giving hospitality to the newly-arrived.

Racial discrimination is not always about angry mobs and violent persecutions. Those are the extreme manifestations of long-term, systemic discrimination. It is the quiet, well-established acceptance of bias, of viewing "the other" as a being of lesser value. It is the white farmers hiring a crew of fruit pickers and not asking any of their names. Or it is the white townsfolk calling every man with an Asian face "Charlie" or every immigrant by a derogatory epithet related to their ethnicity.

The U.S. federal census of 1910 is one of the clearest examples of society's disregard for the residents in the International District. When I went looking for Yasushi Tanaka in the records of that year, I failed to find him. The nearest candidate is a man recorded by the name "Yonaka" who lists his occupation as a laborer on a farm. This census page lists quite sloppily the residents of an apartment or a hotel building on Maynard Avenue South, at the corner of King Street, in the heart of the International District, what is today Hing Hay Park. The census taker who made the rounds with clipboard in hand did not bother to accurately record the unfamiliar names. A blank line... a partial name, misspelled.... Inked-over corrections... Question marks in the margins... At the bottom of the page is a woman called simply "one person." It is basically a head count of anonymous people who were not deemed important enough to be documented. Or perhaps the lodgers in the building were just as suspicious of a stranger knocking on the doors and asking questions.

Yasushi coming from samurai heritage, he never saw himself the way Americans looked at him. In his own mind, he was an artist and intellectual, a transcendent soul who demanded to be appreciated for his own talents. He could not have imagined the racial hostility that would meet him here.

One example of an immigrant's story is Takuji Yamashita, a Seattle resident. He graduated from law school at the University of Washington and successfully passed the state bar exam. However, he could not be granted a law license or allowed to practice. At the time, only U.S. citizens—specifically *white* U.S.

citizens—could be admitted to the bar. Yamashita filed a lawsuit that went all the way to the Washington State Supreme Court and, in October 1902, he lost. The state's Attorney General held that "...in no classification of the human race is a native of Japan treated as belonging to any branch of the white or whitish race."

Less than a year after Yasushi's arrival, the Russo-Japanese War ended with a decisive Japanese victory to the surprise of many world leaders. The Treaty of Portsmouth, mediated by US President Theodore Roosevelt, ended the conflict. Japan's victory reorganized the balance of power in East Asia and established the country as a major power on the modern world stage. With the war over, Yasushi was no longer in danger of being conscripted into military service. Yet, he had no intention of going back and remained in Seattle as a student pursuing his dreams in the fine arts.

By a stroke of luck, Yasushi had arrived just a few years before the doors of immigration law would have closed in his face. In 1907, President Roosevelt began a series of informal agreements and executive orders to appease rising anti-Japanese sentiments. The so-called Gentlemen's Agreement negotiated with the government of Japan asked for suspending passports to their citizens who intended to emigrate to America as un-skilled laborers, unless such laborers were coming to occupy a formerly-acquired home, to join a parent, spouse, or child, or to assume active control of a previously established farming enterprise. As a separate measure, Roosevelt signed an Executive Order that closed a loophole for anyone seeking entry by another route. "Japanese or Korean laborers, skilled and unskilled, who have received passports to go to Mexico, Canada or Hawaii, and come therefrom, [shall] be refused permission to enter the continental territory of the United States."

Joaquin Miller and Sanctuary in The Hights

YASUSHI REMAINED IN Seattle where he continued to study and practice *dessin* sketching and oil painting for several years. Building upon his exposure to Western-style art from his days in Tokyo, and devouring all of the art books in the Seattle Public Library, he was essentially a self-taught artist who gained most of his knowledge from experimenting on his own.

In the spring or early summer of 1909, Yasushi made a road trip to California with his friend for a self-guided artist's retreat. My only evidence of this trip is a scrap of a letter that he wrote to Imogen Cunningham, reproduced here in entirety:

> Toward evening this is a very quiet place here, the Diment Heights [sic], where we have assiduously lived for a month. Toward evening, also, one feels peculiar bottomlessness here, the Diment Height, the cool, obstinately cool hilltop of picturesque eucalyptus and acacia. Toward evening, again, therefore, we burn weed very noisefully, as Issio suggests, not for breaking the flat monotony, but for overcoming the powerful flatness of the noiseless monotony of the flatly powerful evening.
>
> I have been painting busily producing some. Not the warm yellow sunshine that I care for, but the almost excitingly vibrating blue atmosphere of the colourful Heights that I have been studying carefully.
>
> Issio Kuge has been ill, physically and mentally as well as—phraseology runs—spiritually indeed. He seemed almost "broken into pieces" one day when he came back after meeting several romantic fleshes and poetical bones, if you please, and as I was squeezing tubes against a green canvas that I had been working on, I could easily notice how red he looked. So ridiculously red he looked, indeed, after walking among and through the greens, with some curiously lingering hope that chains him to his eucalyplusian [sic] atmosphere. Fever!—and since that time he has been quite colourless and odourless.

Yasushi concludes the letter with a promise, "Issio is not going to see your father this time—so he wants me to let you know," in reference to Imogen

Cunningham's father who had moved from Seattle to a small town north of San Francisco at some point prior to this.

The location is the rustic estate of poet Joaquin Miller in the hills east of Oakland, California. Miller was an eccentric character at the turn of the 19th and 20th century who dubbed his estate "The Hights" with a deliberate misspelling, and called his own house "The Abbey." He established a literary-artistic commune with a spiritual tone unique to himself. He built several monuments of stone and concrete rubble in honor of California politician John C. Fremont, the poets Robert Browning and Elizabeth Barrett Browning, and a Pyramid to Moses. Today the 500 acres of rustic woodland trails are a popular destination for hiking and sightseeing amid groves of oak, eucalyptus, and redwood trees.

At the turn of the 20th century, well-known writers of the day regularly visited The Hights, including Jack London, Bret Harte, Charles Warren Stoddard, and Ambrose Bierce—the so-called Bohemian Club. They participated in outdoor poetry readings at the Hights's small stone amphitheater known as the Fire Circle or the Writer's Circle.

Although mostly known as a sanctuary for poets, Miller's estate also welcomed painters and sculptors. He had a long-time acquaintance with the Rosetti family and the pre-Raphaelite Brotherhood group of artists.

Miller's estate was also a sanctuary for Japanese immigrants, most notably the poet Yonejirō "Yone" Noguchi, to escape the racial hostility of the surrounding urban areas. The Hights encouraged Japanese to set up their own Walden Pond-like cottages. All were welcome if they met two basic criteria: producing works of art or literature and doing handyman chores around the estate. Miller also acted as a matchmaker, encouraging a number of trans-national relationships by quoting the Rudyard Kipling line in defiance, "Oh, East is East, and West is West, and never the twain shall meet," and he was determined to overcome the barriers of nationality and race.

The Parallel Life of Yasushi's Friend Ichizo "Issio" Kuge

THE LEAF-IN-THE-WIND known as Issio Kuge had spent time at Miller's estate, off-and-on, for several years previously. He is mentioned briefly in 1906 in a Hawaiian newspaper's light-hearted travel piece that describes the poet Joaquin Miller's hospitality. "...he called Kuge, and a gentlemanly little Japanese came forward, to whom I was presented as a gentleman and a poet, with the information that Issio Kuge was a poet also from the land of the chrysanthemum, who had lived here for the past two years, and had taken the little cottage formerly occupied by Yone Noguchi, who had lived with Joaquin seven years, and lately had achieved fame as a poet in the United States and abroad. 'You're fond of the poets, Joaquin,' said I. 'Yes, said he musingly, 'I would not have people close around me who were not poets.'"

Another description of Issio Kuge comes from Elsie Whitaker Martinez, the wife of local artist Xavier Martínez, grew up on a property nearby. Interviewed later in life, she mentioned her teenage flirtations with a Japanese fellow "Kugi"—the name turning a bit fuzzy in her memories of years long past. She described him as a young poet who offered her "reams of beautiful eucalyptus bark on which were inscribed his poems in exquisite Japanese characters." Her father, the novelist Herman Whitaker, disapproved of the flirtations and asked Joaquin Miller to intervene. Elsie Martinez recalled one final parting visit. "He brought his incense pot, and his lyrics must have been heartbreaking from the expressions and the dramatic rendering of them. That was the last time I saw him."

Issio Kuge also caught the eye of Charles Warren Stoddard—the author, world traveler, contributor to the *San Francisco Chronicle*, and co-editor along with Bret Harte of the *Overland Monthly* magazine. Years before, Stoddard had shared a secret love affair with a former poet-in-residence Yone Noguchi before the latter departed for New York City, then London, and later Japan.

Stoddard kept a journal on his visit to The Hights for a few days in 1905, from October 28 to 31. He described meeting Issio Kuge, among others, where he hoped to find a new relationship similar to what he had enjoyed with Yone Noguchi. In fact, Kuge occupied the same bungalow that Noguchi had formerly used.

Stoddard's journal is a peculiar mixture of "Oriental" fetishism, ingrained racism, and condescending congeniality. He writes of his fondness for "brown boys" and of Kuge in particular. "Issio Kuge could give me all the spiritual nourishment I need. I could easily love him. A bodyguard should be some simple bucolic, who knows not the world, or who has the tenderness of a woman. He should bring me my mail or any daily papers... make my bed and me comfortable, and cook. Yes, to make it perfect... cook!"

Stoddard frequently uses the derogatory term "Jap" to refer to Issio Kuge and others, in spite of his affections for Yone Noguchi and his expressions of fondness for Kuge in the journal. He describes him as, "A young Jap, Kuge, with a complexion of ivory as with the look of Destiny or fatality in it—his teeth rather large, and beautifully white, his gums like a rose petal—met us at the gate and made himself formally agreeable. His figure is slight tho' not ungraceful." He drops the racial epithet casually, from a place of privilege, without giving a second thought to how a Japanese person might feel offended. For example, "We're all enjoying ourselves as the Japs are chopping wood as if it were child's play." Another example, "After dinner, the Jap boys and I went out to see the young moon in a haze."

Stoddard only spent a few days at Joaquin Miller's estate, but evidently Issio Kuge made a favorable impression. The two continued corresponding for several years afterwards, however, as fate would have it, Stoddard and Kuge never met again.

In a letter dated November 21, 1905, Kuge thanks Stoddard for the gift of a book and expresses a rather melancholy mood. Enclosed with the letter (transcribed verbatim from the original with grammatical errors intact) were two dried pressed leaves and a portrait photograph of himself perusing a book.

> "I think sometime let you humor my ideas on such a perfect work but, I say nothing here, only I enclosed a fallen leaflet...which may tell you mine fate and heart better than I do self, so probably you listen this! Well now, as your hugs, I send lowest picture, will you take? Please accept best wish to yourself, or now and then, would I hear you?

> P.S. Expect I will start away for Ancient Albion very soon because I am living quite unpleasantly here upon the Heights. Please never write about me on any magazine. I should be a nameless fallen leaflet!"

However, Kuge stayed through the winter and in April 1906 he experienced the great San Francisco earthquake. In return, Stoddard wrote letters to his "beloved Issio," worried for his safety after hearing the news of the earthquake, and invited him to come south and live with him in Monterey, California.

Instead of accepting Stoddard's offer, in July 1906, Issio Kuge wrote an affectionate good-bye letter to Stoddard on the eve of sailing home to Japan.

> "Dear Sir: With throbbing heart, I take up my pen. Oh sorry! Since after I have suffered by the ill and now one lung is not well, so in a few days I am going toward Japan to have some medical attendances that seems [to] me quite better than stay here.
>
> Of course if I could recover myself I will come back again to America next spring and live together in such a home as you said ever.
>
> You know how it please me and I wish very much to do so!
>
> Dear Sir, I have lots of things which I must tell you, but my feel about broken up from the sorrow to leave memorable America and I can not write more there.
>
> I think, however, I should pen to you very often when I am in my native place. Now will you wait till then?
>
> Your Little One, Issio Kuge"

Kuge wrote another letter to Stoddard, four months later, Nov 12, 1906, from where he was staying in Japan.

> "Dear Sir:

Your affectionate letter came few days ago. I thank you very much for remembering me still so kindly. Oh too bad, I could have not any chance to write you that I was afraid the letter never reach in Saratoga.

Since from such a fate I have disappointed and wrecked myself awful! B—but lately

The health recovering quite better strong than before living kind happy here.

Yes Sir, if I could, I am going back again to California next February. I say I should like that splendid scene of Monterey also to stay there indeed!

Now through our country it is the harvest time of beautiful rices or fruits, the farmers are very busy with their sickles in the field. You know our this season in a year is most poetic."

Destiny had other plans for Kuge, and despite his promises and well-meaning intentions, he did not return to California after all. He stayed with his uncle in Oita, Japan until the following August 1907, and sailed out of Yokohama on the S.S. *Minnesota* bound for Seattle. During this time period, I assume, Kuge reunited with his friend Yasushi Tanaka.

Kuge did not write another letter to Charles Stoddard for close to two years, when returned to visit briefly at The Hights. By now, Stoddard's health was failing, and this would be the last letter from Kuge in the old poet's collection of papers. Stoddard died at his home in Monterey, California roughly a month after the date (March 12, 1909) on Kuge's final letter.

"Dear Master,

Indeed, I wonder, how this letter may surprise you. Have you ever expect to hear such a news, that still your "little one" is living on the earth?

I am with Joaquin Miller present, I returned from Nippon about one year & half ago and have been in Seattle, lately, I just few days ago I arrived here.

Since I left America I was so long delay to you, but you will allow me, will you not?

The lantern of my life was burning out very near; what can I tell now exact, you know the things on me were quite hard last three, four years; however am trying in the right side, rather I would have done it so.

Here only I wish I could see you once someday before I leave the Heights, why I am going back again to the far north very soon.

Well if you ever could come down to San Francisco, there we'll meet each other and have nice talk of the lots things after we parted.

Your Sincere Little One, Issio Kuge"

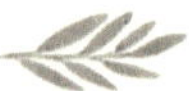

The Parallel Tale of Takeshi Kanno and Gertrude Boyle

BACK WHEN HE HAD VISITED Joaquin Miller's estate and met Issio Kuge, Charles Stoddard also encountered a Japanese fellow named Takeshi Kanno for whom he felt no attraction. Stoddard wrote in his journal, "I care less for Kanno, for he has the air of a Protestant convert, which attracts me not. Issio is a pure Buddhist, how much fairer in spirit and in truth. Issio - I can embrace; Takeshi - I cannot." Also mentioned in the journal is Stoddard's surprise at how the Japanese residents of Miller's estate were already well educated. "Issio Kuge and Takeshi Kanno were talking very intelligently of the musical dramas of Wagner, having seen several of them. Also of Tolstoy, another Russian author now popular in the Japanese tongue. 'We can whip the Russians,' said Kanno, 'but we have no Tolstoy.' They quote Rabbie Burns,

Longfellow, Wordsworth, and many other authors correctly in English; know much of foreign - to them - history as biography; are much better informed in English and American literature than the fellows who used to be in my class at the Catholic University."

Two years after Stoddard's visit, Takeshi Kanno made headlines by courting and marrying a white American woman. Gertrude Boyle was an American sculptor known for her portrait busts of notable celebrities including: the dancer Isadora Duncan, the presidents Teddy Roosevelt and Franklin D. Roosevelt, the naturalist John Muir, the philanthropist Luther Burbank, and the renowned scientist Albert Einstein. Ms. Boyle was commissioned by the eccentric poet Joaquin Miller to sculpt a portrait of his mother, which brought her to Miller's bucolic home in the hills near Oakland, California.

Takeshi Kanno wrote lengthy poems to her, in English, and in return she sculpted a likeness of his head. Boyle and Kanno sought a marriage license in San Francisco but were refused. They widened their quest to the surrounding cities, and failing to find anyone who would sanction their union, they traveled north. They married on May 22, 1907 in Seattle, Washington and returned to the Oakland hills to live in a bungalow on Miller's estate.

The *San Francisco Call* newspaper published a full-page spread to profile (or, more accurately, publicly ridicule) their courtship and marriage. The article characterizes Boyle as an intrepid explorer, "a person who has been endowed by nature with utter fearlessness and love of peril." What seems to us 100 years later to be a perfectly ordinary marriage of a poet and artist, regardless of their national origins, back in 1907 was an astonishing event. The article calls their romance "strange" and "odd." It opens with a ridiculously bizarre, fear-mongering paragraph: "Would you, if you were an American girl and had married a Japanese nobleman—would you sail for Japan on your honeymoon if your girlfriends assured you that your haughty relations in law would chop your head off on your arrival; if they tearfully begged you not to put yourself into the clutches of oriental nobility by the intrusion of a Caucasian; if they assured you that the sweetest greetings of your baronial bridegroom meant merely a fearful and lingering death?"

This is the social climate where Yasushi Tanaka found himself as a young man coming to marriageable age. Immigration from China and Japan remained at a near standstill, and most of those who had come to the U.S. as railroad workers or farm labor were men. He observed his friend Issio Kuge becoming the object of an old man's fetishism. He witnessed his fellow countrymen, like Takeshi Kanno, enduring legal barriers and ridicule at their marriages to American women. If he had wished to pursue a relationship with Imogen Cunningham, she chose to marry the artist Roy Partridge. So, until he met Louise Cann, the bachelor Yasushi devoted himself whole-heartedly to his art.

Tadama Art School

IN THE 1910S, YASUSHI'S life path intersected with an immigrant who came to Seattle from the opposite side of the world. Fokko Tadama was born in India to a Dutch father and an Indonesian mother. Tadama received his training at the Academy of Fine Arts, Amsterdam and the Rijks Museum School of Art, in addition to private instruction in Holland. Tadama had a successful painting career selling Dutch seascapes, however, his wife suffered from acute psychological disorders and had to be institutionalized. Distraught by his wife's mental illness, Tadama left his native country to begin a new life elsewhere. He traveled through Paris and New York, arriving in Seattle around 1910. Leveraging his European exhibition history, he held his first one-man show in Seattle in 1913 at the Seattle Public Library, which was extremely well received by the community. The following year, he started the Fokko Tadama Art School in Seattle that would become an important starting point for many of the city's better-known artists, especially those who had come from Asian countries.

During his rise in the Seattle art scene, Yasushi also made the acquaintance of Frederick C. Torrey, an art dealer with the San Francisco gallery of Vickers, Atkins & Torrey. The two formed a long-term friendship and would continue to correspond for more than a decade. Torrey supported him by acquiring paintings, providing some financial assistance, and gifting reference books to further Yasushi's self-driven art education.

Yasushi's early works featured seascapes and woodland landscapes in the Pacific Northwest. He also made photo-realistic portraits in oil, in pastel, and *dessin* style pen-and-ink or charcoal sketches. He experimented with Futurism and Cubism, with light, shadow, and brilliant variations in color. However, inspired by the growing movement of avant-garde artists seeking expression of the free natural form, and emboldened by Imogen Cunningham's photographs of unclothed figures posed in outdoor settings, Yasuhi turned his attention to painting nudes.

Yasushi applied to present his works at the Panama-Pacific International Exposition to be held in San Francisco in 1915. The prestigious event, stretched along two and a half miles of waterfront property, highlighted San Francisco's grandeur and celebrated the successful completion of the Panama Canal. Millions of visitors strolled the newly-constructed boulevards, along what is today's Fisherman's Wharf. They attended scientific and educational presentations such as wireless telegraphy, telephones, and automobiles. They traveled the world virtually through international pavilions and enjoyed displays of sports, music, and arts. One hundred years later, the Palace of Fine Arts and the Legion of Honor museums continue the legacy of this spectacular event.

Jury selection of the artwork to represent Seattle began in the fall of 1914. At first, Yasushi was refused entry to the Exposition's fine arts exhibit because of his reputation for scandalous nudes, but he persevered. With the personal support of Fokko Tadama and members of the Seattle Fine Arts Society, he managed to get selected into the exhibition with two paintings "The Shadow of the Madrona" and "Misty Evening," neither of which are nudes.

Yasushi also leveraged his rising prominence in Seattle to advertise giving art lessons. This shows that, within a few years of his arrival, he was more of a colleague of Fokko Tadama rather than a student or protégé. Thus, with his prominence as an artist validated by participation in a world-class event, Yasushi continued exhibiting his original works through the sponsorship of the Seattle Fine Arts Society.

The same year as the Pan-Pacific Expo, Yasushi was the headline artist at an exhibit with associates including his own students in Seattle. The brochure includes a detailed list of the paintings on exhibit, by title, and a lengthy essay on his philosophy of art. He writes, in part, "When our intellect awoke we came to know why we paint: we paint in order that we may live consciously, but not merely to exist in painting, nor simply because we have to paint for some means; we learned how to live in Art which is one of those great natural forces manifested in mankind, the everlasting universal religion which has its basis in its very core. We are, in fact, verifying the higher mode of human existence."

Reviews in the local newspapers either gave praise or condemnation, showing the divisiveness between the art community and post-Victorian society at large.

One newspaper reviewer writes: "His 'Last Ray', an impressionistic sea-scape, is an exquisite color poem—a spill of yellow light that is truly luminous across water and low rocks. Rich, curious hues of red, green and dull blue give value to the stream of sunshine. That Mr. Tanaka's work invites serious study is evidenced by the many persons who have visited the gallery since the pictures were hung. Those who are students of Bergson and Eucken and the newer literature in art feel it to be significant that an artist isolated from the insurgent centers, such as Paris and New York, should display such radicalism as this artist shows."

On the other hand, another newspaper spoke in the voice of a morally outraged citizen: "Whoops, my dear! Horrors! Have you seen the paintings of Yasushi Tanaka and 'his independent associates,' at the public library? Speaking very, very soft-pedalish, some of them are a bit risqué, and one of them, 'The Bather,' has 'September Morn' looking like a fully clad, abashed spinster. Women have complained to Chief Lang and the matter has been reported to the city censorship board."

Not everyone in town was offended, however. In particular, one Miss Louise Gebhard Cann wrote a lengthy review and opinion piece for *The Town Crier*, titled "The Way It Affects One." As her exposition goes on at some length, I have transcribed just the first two paragraphs to give a sense of it. "In studying the cubistic work of Mr. Tanaka, I have been impressed by the liberation of spirit conferred by the grasping of its actualities. In 'The Moon,' 'At the Height,' 'Low Tide,' and kindred pictures for the crowd, I find myself at the edge of vast distances; I am invaded by the loneliness of the human who stands in solitude on the sea-shore. This loneliness of the human atom in the vastness of nature penetrates me with a sensuous reverie unendurably beautiful, for it recalls innumerable moments of poignant joy in the world of nature when the subtle, intricate loveless and the majesty of nature reduced me to a small, blindly worshipping, helpless being."

Louise and Yasushi's Courtship and Marriage

SIX MONTHS PASSED FROM Louise Cann first hearing Yasushi's public lecture at the Seattle Fine Arts Association in September 1914 to actually meeting him. As a regular contributor to an events column in the local newspaper, she approached him for an interview. Their romance sparked in that first face-to-face conversation. His experimental style of painting enthralled her, and in turn, her writings fascinated him. Yasushi and Louise saw each other as soul mates, as artistic spirits who conversed on a creative intellectual plane. Their shared philosophies transcended the confines of their physical beings along with the restrictions of Victorian societal norms.

Louise published an essay in a literary journal *The Little Review* titled, "Let Them Fight it Out!" basically saying that art should be for art's sake, not illustrative of contemporary political issues or used as propaganda for social justice movements. This piece gives an early, unfiltered view of her philosophy, as well. "I notice that all my socialist and anarchist friends hold a similar view, one going so far as to declare in the course of an argument on art with a well-known etcher that his etchings could not live because they did not portray the struggles of the masses. Being in principle an anarchist myself, and sympathetic towards much of socialism, I cannot speak as an antagonist to these people but as one of their number who sees that on this point of art's purpose they are mistaken.... But art reduced to illustration of class struggle, bound in service to mere social consciousness, will soon turn sterile and will fail to inspire even those it serves."

During their three-year courtship, Louise spent more and more time at his studio. Once again disregarding scandal, this divorced woman happily modeled semi-nude for Yasushi's paintings. The first piece to go on public exhibit, titled "Blue Cat," portrayed her clad in a silky blue kimono, as described by a newspaper article as, "...gazing at the artist with the expression...of the feline in her eyes. Miss Cann says that it is Tanaka's opinion that there is a little of the cat in every woman; that desire, as she put it, to purring when fondled and to scratch when stroked the wrong way." This painting and these published comments caused outrage from the conservative citizens, as it portrayed a new image of womanhood. No longer a delicate Victorian flower, or a passive object of men's sexual desires, the Blue Cat unabashedly realized her own desires. The message in her eyes said, stroke me nicely but watch out for the claws.

Meanwhile, Louise's father Judge Cann had been in failing health for several years. His illness worsened after Louise returned from New York and divorced her husband. In the fall of 1915, Judge Thomas Cann ended his own life at age 82. Rather than die of natural causes at home, surrounded by his loving family, he chose to take a solitary stroll out his front door on the afternoon of Monday, October 25, 1915. He did not go very far. Only 200 feet away, he sat down and swallowed a bottle of carbolic acid. When evening came and he had not returned home, the neighbors searching with lanterns discovered his body. In his coat pocket were two letters of farewell—one to his wife and one to an undisclosed friend. The contents of the letters were never revealed to the media, except that on the outside of the envelope, he had written, "Worse this morning, October 25. No chance for recovery."

Yasushi continued to correspond with San Francisco art dealer Frederick Torrey. In a letter dated June 16, 1915, he explains at length his purposeful approach to art. "Through philosophical studies of Kant and psychological and metaphysical researches, I believe I can clearly explain my art which is nothing but the artistic reason in its purity that can take any free form in the art of plastic and graphic expression. Kant's a priori synthesis principle has a great deal to do with this on the ground of the matter and form. Consideration of space, of pure perception and the conceptual space of imagination in connection with empirical perception enables us to actualize the reality or any imaginative reality in some certain form of artistic representation upon flat planes."

In this letter he also mentions his growing affection for "Miss Louise Cann, the writer who has been writing for the *Literary Digest* and several other prominent magazines. She is from Cornell, and herself is an artist of strikingly radical type. I am sending you her criticism which appeared partly in the *Town Crier*. I deeply regret to say that the editor took off all her important discussion about the new philosophy concerning Bergson and Eucken in relation to the new movement of art." He ends with mentioning, "My friend Kuge has gone to New York and Miss Cann has just saved me from starvation in this desert of thoughts. I am expecting to join Kuge in New York in [the] near future."

So, in just ten short years from his arrival in Seattle, Yasushi Tanaka had established himself in the local art scene as a visionary artist as well as a teacher and public lecturer. Yasushi's art style is unique, a conglomerate and reinterpretation of experimenting with styles, of cubism's futuristic shapes, or the realistic portraits, borrowing concepts from Cezanne, Whistler, and Kandinsky. Always hungry for growth and expression of his individual ideas, having emerged from a modernizing Japan that, in one generation sprang from the 17th century into the 20th, Yasushi embodied the young men of his age rushing into a modern era.

Yet, unlike his white colleagues in the Seattle art community, he faced discrimination for being Japanese that limited the opportunities to advance his career. Having already incurred the wrath of Seattle's conservative art critics, he would soon commit a bigger scandal by marrying a woman of another race.

Local newspapers erupted after Yasushi and Louise got married on November 23, 1917 at the Seattle courthouse. The Justice of the Peace Otis W. Brinker performed the marriage ceremony reluctantly, and only after the couple managed to convince him that their relationship was based on true love and a spiritual connection. One of the witnesses to the civil ceremony, Suego Sasabe, was a Japanese resident of Seattle and also married to a German wife. They had four daughters and professed to the judge that they were very happy. With this testimony of another inter-racial marriage as evidence, the judge reluctantly agreed.

"Our art lives have united us," Louise Gebhard Cann told her local newspapers in defense of marrying Yasushi Tanaka, a Japanese immigrant. "We live on the same planes of thought; and ours is one of the true marriages—which means much more than merely a wedding ceremony." Louise described their marriage as a cosmic mating of minds. Coming from opposite shores of the Pacific Ocean, they had independently formed similar philosophies of modernity and craved the freedom of artistic expression. These two adventurers shared a vision of a brighter future that discarded the oppressive, stale traditions of the past. It was destiny, or simple luck, that they found each other.

Yasushi and Louise married while World War I raged in Europe, about a year before the signing of the armistice. Perhaps they felt a sense of urgency to transcend the global epidemic of division and hatred in the "war to end all wars." Alongside their wedding announcement and interviews in the local newspapers are headlines describing the horrific carnage in France and Germany. Tsar Nicolai II abdicated to the revolutionary forces earlier in the year ending the rule of monarchs in Russia forever. The homeland of Louise's maternal grandparents turned itself inside-out with rapid changes to geopolitical boundaries; the lands of Bavaria and Prussia would soon be forever changed.

Closer to home, the Great War was not the only source of division and hatred that Yasushi and Louise had to face. The anti-Asian sentiment on the Pacific coast had risen steadily since the Gold Rush days of her father's generation. Along with the increase in population with Chinese laborers brought for construction of railroad lines, and the influx of other immigrants from overseas, came resentment from the white citizens. Frontier men like Louise's father had fresh in their minds the trek across the continent and their struggles to achieve statehood. The white population very much carried the pioneer mentality of colonizers who decimated the native population and somehow claimed the entire west coast of North America as their own. In their minds was the exclusive privilege of ownership, disregarding any thought of giving legitimacy to their non-white neighbors who had also journeyed from afar to settle on the same shores.

U.S. federal laws on immigration, like the Chinese Exclusion Act of 1882, restricted unskilled laborers from coming to the U.S. but did not quell the violent race riots of the 1870s and 1880s. If any, the increasingly restrictive laws only fanned the flames of racial intolerance by giving license to nationalists. Since the U.S. federal government had singled out Chinese to be excluded, the white citizens felt emboldened to express prejudice against all Asians—whether Chinese or not.

Louise Cann risked more than social stigma and ridicule for marrying a Japanese man. According to the Expatriation Act of 1907, any American man immediately conferred U.S. citizenship onto a foreign wife but an American woman relinquished her U.S. citizenship by marrying a foreign husband.

Several years after Louise and Yasushi's marriage, with passage of The Married Woman's Citizenship Act in 1922, the U.S. reformed its immigration policy. Thousands of American-born women married to foreign-born men before the 1920s had to file applications to regain their lost citizenship. Even so, that new rule would not be universally applied. Other restrictions targeted at immigrants from East Asia made Yasushi ineligible to apply for U.S. citizenship by any means. Japanese immigrants were not allowed to become naturalized citizens of the U.S. until after World War II, with the McCarran-Walter Act signed in 1952.

Louise likely received condemnation from polite Seattle society although she does not voice her complaints in the newspaper interviews. She praises the open-minded acceptance of their acquaintances and neighbors. By omission, she does not mention her own family's opinion. The public face she presented seems to be a creature of isolation striving for a higher intellectual and spiritual awareness. By marrying Yasushi, she had joined with her soul mate—full steam ahead and damn the consequences.

Yasushi continued to produce artwork prolifically during their honeymoon years. He filled every available inch of space with canvases and easels, sketchpads and charcoal pencils, jugs of turpentine and tubes of oil paint. In between exhibiting his original artwork, he gave lessons to several students and did work-for-hire portraits of local personalities to pay the bills.

The *Seattle Star* newspaper published an interview with Louise Cann in Yasushi's home studio. Along with her eloquent defense of Yasushi characterizing women as cats, this is a rare description of his workspace. "Louise Gebhard Cann, author and model for Tanaka's queer portrait, welcomed the non-believer to the studio at 917 Seneca Street, with a feline's regard for comfort by placing a chair near a blazing grate fire. She herself languidly drooped comfortably on a short stool in the robe in which Tanaka had painted her." The article continues: The proverbial tiger rug, crowned by a pile of pillows, was graced by a smiling woman. Sketches of nude figures, children and matrons were piled in confusion in the corners. Cubistic studies were hung on the walls. Half finished oils rested on easels... Color was rampant everywhere—a blue of colors, which Miss Cann explained was the semi-sensuous impression of an interesting woman... Places for tea and things occupied another room. Good books were to be found, but everywhere an atmosphere of work—hard, worthwhile work—and the model filled the place with a feline grace that was more understandable after the short visit."

His studio space in a building at 917 Seneca Street was also his residence. The building occupied the city block adjoining the corner of Spring and Terry

Streets, in an area of the city known as First Hill, near where the photographer Imogen Cunningham lived and worked with her husband Roi Partridge in a cottage remodeled into an artists' studio.

The Tanakas had a close relationship with Ms. Cunningham both as next-door neighbors and as colleagues at the Seattle Fine Arts Society. It appears they read the same philosophy and futurist literature popular among the intellectuals of the time, including the poetry of Yone Noguchi. Ms. Cunningham advocated modernist ideas in her compositions and she wrote essays of her opinions to photographic magazines. She blazed the trail of unconventionality by her courage in photographing nudes, at first in ethereal, pre-Raphaelite style poses and later in unabashed clarity. Before Yasushi had exhibited paintings of nudes, Ms. Cunningham had caused her own scandal in town by daring to publish in the *Town Crier* artistic photographs of her husband Roi Partridge posing in outdoor settings fully nude.

Ms. Cunningham wrote letters to her husband Roi Partridge, while he was traveling away from home to make sketches of Mount Rainier. On the subject of being invited to exhibit her photographs in galleries in New York, she mentions Yasushi Tanaka and Louise Cann by name. "What else shall I send? I think I'll get busy & do a shocker—Miss C. suggests today that I photograph her nude with Tanaka dressed—I have an idea—guess I'll get busy." A few days later she wrote another letter to her husband: "...I photographed Gryff [her toddler son] with Miss Cann indoors and somewhat nude...At best the proposition of photographing a mother and child is liable to be either sentimental or absolutely unpictorial but what I wanted to get to-day was a portrait of Gryff and something of him nude with a woman as background."

Unfortunately, whatever photographs Ms. Cunningham took of the Tanakas are forever lost due to a destructive housekeeper who caused house fires that damaged her collection of glass-plate negatives. Further destruction of inventory came at the hands of Ms. Cunningham herself who, upon vacating the cottage a year later, dismantled her own studio and smashed the majority of her glass-plate negatives because they were too bulky and heavy to transport.

The Seattle Fine Arts Society's Imogen Cunningham and her husband Roi Partridge left Seattle for Oakland, California in September 1917, just one month before the Tanakas held their wedding. Ms. Cunningham was able to be with her father in his final years. Partridge taught at Mills College and, later in the 1920s, became the director of the college's art museum that would exhibit the works of Ansel Adams, Imogen Cunningham, and others.

Without Imogen Cunningham's support in the Seattle Fine Arts Society, Yasushi's next few years became less hospitable. He produced roughly one hundred paintings in this period but constantly struggled to gain a foothold in the gallery scene.

To their credit, but also to their detriment, Yasushi and Louise refused to play the smiling, hand-shaking game to gain favors. Instead, they engaged in a public feud with Seattle's conservative art critics, most notably Mrs. Adele M. Ballard, one of Seattle's prominent bourgeois citizens. The widow of Mr. John G. Ballard wrote a regular, weekly column called "With the Fine Arts Folk" for *The Town Crier* magazine. She frequently published stinging reviews of Yasushi's exhibitions, saying he lacked "the fundamentals, the knowledge of anatomy." Ballard took jabs at his credentials by writing, "Mr. Tanaka has not received in the art centers of the country the recognition that has been given several other Seattle artists, yet this city has been generous indeed in its encouragement of his work."

Louise rose to the occasion and defended her husband by publishing positive reviews in defense of her husband's nude paintings. One of her articles appeared in *American Art News* saying, "He has been in Seattle thirteen years, has held many exhibitions here, and on the occasion of each exhibit has had to fight a battle on behalf of freedom for the study of art and the true and sincere expression of that study. Each time he has triumphed against narrow-mindedness and won friends. It may be said truthfully that he has educated the Seattle public."

Louise persisted with a Letter to the Editor of *American Art News* again defending her husband's nude paintings as "...the visual truth of the figure as related to background." She quotes a remark by Frederick Torrey, "...if Mr. Tanaka's work did show defects in "anatomy" and "drawing," they (his critics) wouldn't know it anyhow, for none of them had probably ever in their lives seen a nude figure. The real issue with these ladies was, of course, morality. They are still embarrassed in the presence of realistic life work."

Throughout this period, Louise worked hard to promote her husband's career by using her own talents as a writer. Under the gender-neutral byline of L. Gebhard Cann, she published an in-depth profile of Yasushi Tanaka and his work—including black-and-white reproductions of several paintings—for *The International Studio* magazine in September 1918. "Yasushi Tanaka is to-day one of the most significant personalities on the Pacific slope because he represents, as does no other, the struggle and the triumph of the uncompromising artist in an indifferent art-ignorant community—a community even hostile; he shows the moulding power of the creative mentality on such a community—the helplessness of the latter when attacked by the creative force; he is the most striking development of that new type, the individual transplanted from the environment of one race into that of another entirely different; because he exemplifies, as does no other in this part of the world, the vision one race may bring to another, the concrete deepening of mental life that may result from the fusion of the life and the cultures of two races, and the universality and leadership which necessarily result, in spite of every opposition, when these forces are focused by genius."

Louise's background in journalism, and as a literary critic, gave her the tools to promote Yasushi's career as a full and equal partner in a way that she never could experience with her first husband. Her vigorous, passionate involvement clearly helped to bring Yasushi's works into the white-dominated art galleries.

Yasushi won second place in the Seattle Fine Arts Society's fifth annual Northwest art competition, as reported in the *Seattle Sunday Times*, March 23, 1919. Hundreds of spectators visited the galleries daily to feast their eyes on the selected winners. First prize went to Paul M. Gustin's "November Twilight" that evoked a feeling of "...a gray and chilly, but not unattractive, scene. Many such scenes and many such days have been encountered by anyone who has lived long on Puget Sound."

Yasushi's painting titled, "Autumn Creek" is described by the newspaper as representing "...a stream and an autumn more characteristic of his native Japan, it would seem, than the Pacific Northwest. Curiously enough, the autumnal tone of the picture is more a quality of the coloring in the stream itself than of the relatively less important glimpses of earth and foliage that enter into the composition of this work. The outstanding achievement is in the stream. Here short strokes—literally dashes—are used for a kaleidoscopic alternation and juxtaposition of colors which do not actually commingle. Dashes of green, dashes of blue, dashes of purple, dashes of red and dashes of brown all inter into the representation of this placid little stream. The onlooker finds in the water the feeling usually sought for in the changing leaves of trees and shrubs. This painting hangs on the east wall with a number of other examples of Tanaka's impressionistic brush."

Not every one of Seattle's high-society ladies disapproved of Yasushi as an artist. A number of them contrasted Mrs. Ballard and the closed-minded, provincial attitudes of those who objected to Tanaka's modernistic style paintings.

Seattle's newly established chapter of the Jack London Club was a charitable organization inspired by the San Francisco-based author of *Call of the Wild*, and a lesser known story *Michael—Brother of Jerry*, the tale of a dog brutally mistreated by its trainer. The club encouraged activism against animal cruelty, their most effective and well-known tactic being audience walkouts of performances such as circuses that exploited animals as entertainment.

A gala event to celebrate the Jack London Club's Seattle chapter took place at the Hotel Washington over three days, beginning January 15, 1920. Mrs. Erastus Brainerd, the wife of a former editor of the *Post-Intelligencer* newspaper, was in charge of the membership booth. The newspaper reports that 3,000 private invitations were issued.

Yasushi exhibited a painting titled, "The Black Lily" for sale—proceeds going to the benefit of the Jack London Club. The fairly conventional-style portrait of an unnamed woman depicted her in a dark dress and a saucy pose reminiscent of the opera Carmen.

Another of Yasushi's paintings exhibited at this same event was an oil portrait of a dog named Ponto. The stray dog had become a celebrity in the headlines of local papers a few months earlier as a light-hearted human interest story. The members of the Jack London Club named Ponto their mascot and decided to make the pup's face their insignia. Yasushi's realistic portrait of the Irish Setter was copied onto campaign buttons and other ephemera to promote the club.

Another moment of acceptance came with the local Red Cross acquisition of Yasushi's oil portrait of an American soldier during World War I. The model for the portrait, Edward C. Braden, was also a pupil of Yasushi's art school and showed promise as an artist in his own right. In Mrs. Ballard's stinging review of Yashushi's works in *The Town Crier*, she mentions, "Several pencil drawings by one of his pupils, E. C. Braden, stand out well and show character. One of this man's paintings is hung facing the entrance and carries well..."

Louise arranged for the Red Cross to display the portrait of Braden, most likely through her sister-in-law Edna True Cann, a volunteer with the Seattle chapter of the Red Cross who spear-headed clothing donations for needy refugees in the European regions and other activities to support the war effort. My assumption is that Louise had reached out to her brother's wife as a prominent volunteer for the Red Cross to arrange hanging the soldier's portrait for their headquarters. Perhaps it was a gesture of patriotism and charity on Louise's part, or perhaps it was a more practical marketing effort to gain legitimacy in the conservative circles of Seattle's society.

Reaching beyond the confines of Seattle's narrow-mindedness, Yasushi and Louise expanded their circle of acquaintances to international travelers. The Tanakas frequently hosted small dinner parties at their home studio at 917 Seneca Street, as mentioned in the newspaper society pages. Among the more notable of their visitors and acquaintances, Rabindranath Tagore was the first non-European to win (in 1913) the Nobel Prize in Literature. He promoted forward-thinking ideas that inspired many well-known poets such as William Butler Yeats. Tagore traveled the world extensively around the turn of the century, spreading his philosophy of universality—that human-defined divisions were superficial. He was an ardent anti-nationalist at the time when global nationalism was on the rise.

Another world-renowned acquaintance, Vilhjalmur Stefansson, was the American son of Icelandic immigrants. He is mainly remembered as an explorer of the Arctic Polar regions in the early 20th century. He spent considerable time in Alaska with the Inuit people as an ethnologist and published several books on the subject.

Stefansson commissioned a portrait from Yasushi that is profiled in the *Seattle Sunday Times*, October 12, 1919. The newspaper article, byline anonymous, inserts opinions that are overtly, unashamedly racist. "When the Norwegian explorer, Vilhjalmur Stefansson, sat for his portrait this summer to Seattle's Japanese artist, Yasushi Tanaka, what were Tanaka's reactions to the man of the North, his opposite? The Viking from the long nights of Iceland interpreted by the *ekaki* (artist) from the Land of the Rising Sun! What does the Oriental, whose latent art instincts are founded on the tactful drawing of a spray of bamboo on silk, think of the Scandinavian, the man of sinews and endurance, as a subject for his painting?"

In this same article, Yasushi explained his attitude towards portraiture. "The idea of painting a portrait—nothing but a portrait—is detestable to me. I don't consider it a high art. As an art-work, a true portraiture is interesting for the reason that through technique the painter can penetrate into the inner being of the sitter. It is not that knowledge of the inner being we obtain through acquaintance or friendship that enables the painter to paint a successful portrait; but the knowledge that comes from an impression on the artist's eye at the moment of meeting with the sitter. The artist constructs a form which will respond to this visual impression."

As soon as World War One ended, the Spanish Flu pandemic raged in the country. The city of Seattle also suffered but fared better than many other cities. Early intervention of the city's health commissioner enforced the wearing of flu masks, voluntary quarantine of the residents, and a short-term lockdown of all church services, theaters, poolrooms, libraries, entertainment in cafes and restaurants, and public schools. Any businesses allowed to remain open were required to prevent crowding. In the end, Seattle's influenza epidemic claimed over 1,400 lives from September 1918 through February 1919, and left the city with an excess death rate of 414 per 100,000—roughly half the excess death rate of Pittsburgh.

Emerging from these dark days, and with mounting opposition from the busy-bodies of Seattle society, the Tanakas made the decision to seek their opportunities elsewhere.

The Arctic explorer Vilhjalmur Stefansson did the favor of carrying a number of Yasushi's paintings to New York and made great efforts to arrange a gallery showing—without success. New York's modern art museums were likewise unreceptive. As a last resort, the paintings were exhibited privately at the Natural History Museum. This came as a disappointment for Yasushi who had been hoping to advance his career beyond Seattle's limitations.

Another career setback occurred when the Corcoran Gallery of Art, a prestigious art museum in Washington D.C., had invited Yasushi for their seventh contemporary American painters exhibit. The Corcoran later withdrew the invitation for the reason that he was not considered a truly

American painter simply because he was born overseas. It must have seemed that, from coast to coast, the doors of opportunity slammed in his face.

Finances continued to be an issue. The Pacific Northwest offered a limited marketplace for selling his artwork to private collectors. Teaching art lessons to the residents of Seattle who could afford him, on the heels of World War I and the Spanish flu pandemic, offered very limited opportunity. Louise had no family to rely on, financially or otherwise, and so the Tanakas lived virtually hand-to-mouth every day.

Yasushi explained their situation in a letter to Frederick Torrey dated February 9, 1920: "It was last summer that luck knocked at my door. I and my works were introduced to one of the Japanese collectors who came to the city from San Francisco. He truly appreciated my paintings and bought six paintings at once at my own price. A few other sales followed and I am now very well "fixed," as to speak, after a hard struggle for some satisfactory material gain. Louise and I enjoyed our summer trip, first time in the history of my life, to the San Juan Islands, which enabled me to paint thirty fair-sized sketches in three weeks. We liked the rocks and water, the blue gray summer evenings and the cool green moonlight."

In the same letter, Yasushi mentions that his old friend Issio Kuge had been "waiting for me" by renting a studio in New York City, at 421 E. 58th Street, for more than six months. Unfortunately, that Sutton Place neighborhood at the foot of the Queensboro Bridge was doomed to be bulldozed and redeveloped into luxury residences. Mr. Sutton's struggling venture was saved by the arrival of the millionaires Vanderbilt and Morgan in 1920, which began the neighborhood's transformation into a wealthy enclave. One can easily assume that with gentrification came the displacement of the existing tenants. Today, that address is a parking garage beneath newly-constructed luxury condominiums. So, with my assumption that the residents of 421 E. 58th Street were evicted in the name of progress, the dream of an artists' studio evaporated, and Yasushi's friend Issio Kuge once again became a vagabond poet on the road.

Considering the setbacks in gaining a foothold in the New York art scene, and with the impending loss of the studio space that Kuge had been occupying, the Tanakas changed their goals and decided instead to go on to Paris.

Yasushi and Louise held their farewell exhibition of over one hundred paintings in January 1920 at the Seattle Fine Arts gallery. They hoped to sell enough artwork to raise funds for the move. As described after the fact in *American Art News*, "The show consisted mainly of life-size standing portraits, large decorative panels, figure pieces, screens, landscapes, and followed an exhibit of small paintings, chiefly San Juan Island shorescapes in the Schneider gallery. Most of the canvases in both collections had not before been shown, and represented work of the last year and a half." The titles are given in the brochure but no accompanying photos. It's always hard to match his titles with his work, or dates, as he never signed the back of his canvases.

In the public eye, the event is touted as a success. Behind the scenes, however, Yasushi's letter to Frederick Torrey, February 9, 1920, told a different story.

> I held my large exhibition of one hundred paintings in the gallery of the Fine Arts last month. It was certainly the most successful show that the society has ever had. On account of my well-ordered frames, for which I have spent nearly two thousand dollars at the local frame makers since the year last, the show had an expensive appearance. However, this caused among the public the strict division between the enthusiastic appreciation of my individual art and the haters of my peculiar art stench.
>
> The hostile feeling against me which had been caused by their misapprehension of my independence in my own research went up to the top. The Fine Arts Society itself, as a whole, has been very unfriendly toward us and refused entirely any social affair connected with my exhibit. I was even told that even the issuing of invitations at my own expense would offend the society to the extent that they would close the gallery absolutely.
>
> I could hardly keep my smile as the exhibit was originally planned by my enthusiastic friends. The society did their best to "kill" the show, the most foolish thing they could do. It certainly amused me to think that the society was so stirred up that it deliberately took this most miserable step. The point of it all was that they tried to make it absolutely impossible for me to realize any material gain from this

> exhibit. My wife and I uttered nothing but our deep appreciation of the society whose kindness has enabled me to secure the room for the show and kept our smile. Our friends were enraged, but the Town Crier defended the haters of my art declaring that they did not regard me as an artist.
>
> So, just in time, Paris is waiting for us. My desire is only to be a painter, not necessarily an American or a Japanese. I think we have already secured a good studio at Bourg-la-Reine, 20 minutes ride from Paris, through a former student of mine who has written to the owner of the studio, now empty, sometime ago about our going.
>
> I am trying to settle in Paris just as soon as I can and help and encourage my wife for her literary career. I am now dreaming of my hearty dive into my unknown but sure coming art that will in due time crown me not only as an artist but also as an aesthetic space philosopher as well. I am, as you very well know, very much opposed to the idea that art is, and should be, after all, in the picture making, which has for centuries been repeated by the limited mind of mankind. The possibilities existing deeply within unknown space and artistic media for the aesthetic attainment are unlimited. Very few, very very few, realize what the father Cezanne has just started to do. This is the most ecstatic age that artists have ever lived in!

The Tanakas had originally planned to leave for France in March but were delayed for several months by immigration paperwork. The loss of Louise Cann's U.S. citizenship by marriage to a Japanese national had now come back to haunt them. She could no longer apply for an American passport, which typically would have been issued in under a month. As Yasushi briefly explained in his letter to Frederick Torrey, February 9, 1920, "On account of my wife's registration in the Japanese government, it may take more than two months to obtain our passport." When the Tanakas departed the United States, Louise Cann would go to France not as an American but as a Japanese wife.

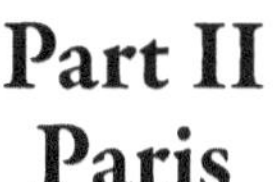

Part II
Paris

Yasushi and Louise sailed out of New York near the end of May 1920 and spent about a week crossing the Atlantic Ocean in a steamship. Most of Yasushi's 100+ paintings had to be left behind in storage in New York, under the care of his friend Issio Kuge, while making arrangements to transport the cargo at a later date.

Paris in the early summer of 1920 was a city coming back to life. Not quite two years after the Armistice that ended World War I—the war to end all wars—Europe had also just emerged from a year of mourning the millions of lives lost in the so-called "Spanish Flu" global influenza pandemic. In America this decade is referred to as the Roaring Twenties but in France they call it the "années folles" or, The Crazy Years. It was a unique moment in history that is romanticized as the era of unbridled creativity, the years when Jazz music became mainstream, when the silent films of Hollywood created movie stars like Rudolph Valentino, Charlie Chaplin, and Douglas Fairbanks. Women cast off their corsets and the last vestiges of Victorian-Era prudishness were swept into the dustbin of history. Countless volumes of historical retrospectives are devoted to this period, immortalizing the names of celebrity artists, musicians, and writers. Paris was known as the City of Light, the ultimate destination and fertile ground for creative artists and intellectuals.

The Tanakas disembarked anonymously on the shores of France and passed before customs inspectors at the famous train station Gare Saint Lazare immortalized by Monet's series of paintings years before. Louise knew French—perhaps from her mother or perhaps from education. She easily conversed on the streets and in cafes, her mind buzzing with excitement to be immersed in centuries of literature and history. Yasushi could not wait to express with paint his pent-up imagination fueled by new sights, new colors, and new sensory experiences. In their own minds, they were not a man and a woman, or a Japanese and an American, but simply Painter and Writer alight with optimism and hope for a fresh start in a new land. Indeed, the City of Light at this moment in history would give them opportunities to realize their full potential that they could not find anywhere else on earth.

The earliest document I have is a letter from Yasushi to the San Francisco art dealer Frederick Torrey, dated July 24, 1920, that describes their excitement and the circumstances of their early days. Their first residence in Paris was a small apartment in the municipal district Montmartre, the location of the famed Moulin Rouge cabaret. Yasushi describes his first impressions of the "old beautiful city full of great arts and human history." He reports, "We are quite happy here, and seem to be inspired every minute by something," and that, "some of those paintings in the Louvre are still kept away somewhere, but everything seems to have been managed after the war. Some paintings and sculptures of the Le Petit Palais which were added after the war are immensely interesting." Also, "since the studio was thoroughly furnished, easels and everything, I at once sat down before the easel and have been working very assiduously since then except two or three days in a week when we go out to see Paris." However, his exuberance is dimmed by financial worries. "The prices of things are certainly dreadfully high. We are paying 800 Frs a month for the studio, and the art materials are just as expensive as in America."

Thriving in the bright summer sunlight of Paris, Yasushi produced a good volume of fresh work right away. By the end of summer, when the lease expired for their temporary apartment, they relocated out of Montmarte to a villa in Bois Colombes—a suburb northwest of Paris. The small villa located at 130 rue Henri Litolff had been recently vacated.

In early January 1921, Louise wrote a letter to Frederick Torrey relaying their new address and updating him on their lives thus far. "The *atelier* is larger than the one we had at Montmarte and very much more convenient for the kind of work Yasushi does. Besides, we have a delightful garden, a real house—and I have my own study—so we are most comfortable.... Yasushi has painted a great deal since coming here—chiefly figure prices. He had a landscape, a draped figure and a nude in the Salon d'Automne. But he feels that he does not care to exhibit in the Salons. He wishes to hold his own show and as soon as the rest of his paintings come from New York we plan to get a gallery.

Two cases of paintings came a month ago and the remaining five should arrive here soon. Then, I suppose, our real battle begins, the battle for a place for the exhibit. Several persons have offered to make the arrangements for us but since we do not know what the connections are, I think I shall try to do everything myself."

Yasushi was not the only Japanese painter seeking to spread his wings in Paris—the global center of the art world. By the late 1920s, more than 1,500 Japanese resided in the city, and roughly a quarter of those were aspiring artists. They attended the prestigious art schools and exhibited their works in the salons along with painters arriving from other European countries.

The concept of an artists' salon began in the 17th century as an annual exhibition of recent graduates of the *École des Beaux-Arts* (School of Fine Arts) as a mark of royal favor. After the turbulent decades following the French Revolution, the salon system underwent a restructuring in the late 19th century with the rise of Impressionism—a new style of painting that had difficulty in gaining acceptance in the traditional salon exhibitions. The *Salon des Refusés* (or, the Salon of the Rejects) that opened in May 1863 contained a selection of works rejected by salons that year and marked the birth of the avant-garde art movement.

In the 1920s, these five Salons were the prestigious, large-scale academic venues for artists to exhibit their works. Membership was essential for an artist to validate legitimacy and reputation in this competitive field. In his career in Paris, Yasushi would become a member of all but the first of these listed below.

1. *Salon des Artistes Francais*, held in the spring at the Grand Palais, was the oldest established, and most conservative in thematic tone
2. *Salon de la Societe Nationale des Beaux-Arts*, held in spring at the Grand Palais, was founded in 1890 after seceding from the Artistes Francais
3. *Salon d'Automne*, held at the Grand Palais, founded in 1903 by the painter Renoir and the sculptor Rodin was the most moderate in thematic tone
4. *Salon des Independants*, with no jury and no prizes, and accessible to all entrants, was the most radical or experimental
5. *Salon des Tuileries*, co-founded in 1923 by painters Albert Besnard

and Bessie Davidson, was also organized in opposition to the official salon system

Yasushi and his fellow countrymen had a peculiar advantage—or disadvantage—by drawing on their national heritage. Japanese motifs in art and fashion raged in popularity with a so-called "japonisme" fad that began decades earlier. Exports of Japanese wood-blocks prints showing quaint scenes of that faraway land enchanted the Europeans to a frenzy. Paper fans and lanterns, silk kimonos, and dishware were imported to every fashion-conscious household.

The French Impressionist artist Claude Monet is most famous for his landscapes and lilies floating in a pond, but he also painted his blonde Camille wife wearing a red kimono. This painting, titled "La Japonaise," is considered by art historians to be Monet's satirical poke at Parisians' fascination with Japan. However, in recent years, it has become a controversial piece. An exhibition of this painting in 2015, at Boston's Museum of Fine Arts, included an interactive activity for museum-goers to try on a replica kimono and take selfies in front of the painting. The museum received a vocal backlash of objections calling the activity racist and a glorification of oriental fetishism.

Yasushi faced a different sort of blatant racism in 1920s Paris than what he had experienced in Seattle. He experienced a façade of acceptance that perhaps reminded him of his brief stay at Joaquin Miller's sanctuary in the California hills. The Europeans gladly appropriated the cultural trappings of Japan—the cherry blossoms and the rice paper—and celebrated the arts and literature. However, they lagged behind in their acceptance of its living, breathing people. Japanese artists like Yasushi faced an invisible wall of their own culture's baggage, pigeonholed in the style of wood-block prints and paper screens. Anyone who dared to paint in the European style received judgement through the lens of racism. The talents of Japanese artists were often praised in art journals but with a disqualifying tagline: very good...for an "Oriental."

The Japanese artists living in Paris in the 1920s were mischaracterized by the author Ernest Hemingway, in his memoir *A Moveable Feast* where he mentions them only briefly, condescendingly, and no one by name. "Japanese artists... were all noblemen where they came from and wore their hair cut long. Their hair glistened black and swung forward when they bowed and I was very impressed by them but I did not like their paintings. I did not understand them but they did not have any mystery, and when I understood them, they meant nothing to me. I was sorry about this but there was nothing I could do about it."

The Fabulous Monsieur Foujita

A DISCUSSION OF THE Paris art scene of the 1920s would be incomplete without mention of Yasushi's more famous contemporary: Tsuguharu Fujita. He altered the spelling of his name in Paris, branding himself as simply "Foujita," but here I refer to his original name.

Until now, he has been all but forgotten and is rarely, if ever, mentioned in histories of 1920s Paris. The artists of European ancestry are household names—Picasso, Cezanne, Rodin, Matisse, and the aging Monet who lived quietly in the countryside. When I began this research project, I read a few contemporary works such as Hemingway's "A Moveable Feast," and "Paris Was Yesterday" a compilation of articles published in *The New Yorker* magazine by Janet Flanner. There is barely a mention of the hundreds of Japanese artists residing in Paris, much less the notorious Fujita.

Fujita bypassed the United States and traveled straight to Paris in 1913 after studying art for some time in Tokyo. He made the acquaintance of a Chilean painter Manuel Ortiz de Zárate who introduced him to Pablo Picasso the legendary painter. Fujita's first solo exhibition, in June 1917 at Gallery Chéron, near the Champs-Élysées, was a commercial triumph. He became a member of the *Salon d'Automne* and quickly rose up the ranks to become a jurist. He later became a member of the *Salon des Tuileries* and was a jurist at the *Beaux-Arts* school. In sitting on the jury of art salons, Fujita was in a unique position to support and showcase his fellow countrymen.

Whereas the other Japanese in Paris stayed within the safe boundaries of conventional subjects, imitating Monet's flowers and Cezanne's landscape, Fujita painted nudes. He developed a unique blend of oil paint, chalk, lead, and magnesium sulfate to create the illusion of ivory skin on canvas. His most famous model, "Kiki de Montparnasse" posed for him frequently as did a young girl named Lucie with skin so pale that he nicknamed her "Yuki" meaning snow in Japanese. Photographic reproductions of his work hardly do them justice, as I understand, the originals are ethereal and luminous.

At the height of the 1920s, Fujita's works were in high demand, exhibited and sold for extravagant prices to international collectors. He was Yasushi's greatest competitor in the marketplace and, in many ways, his polar opposite. Marketing himself as a brand character came naturally and he enjoyed celebrity. He pursued the headlines and published photographs of himself working on oil canvases. His biography *Glory in a Line* gives the overall impression that he was a bold, independent, outspoken man who craved the spotlight.

Fujita gave the world the stereotypical look of a Japanese man that would endure in caricatures for decades to come. His *kappa* style bowl haircut was somewhat childish, reminiscent of Christopher Robin illustrated in the original Winnie-the-Pooh books. His round frame glasses were popularized at the time by the silent film comedian Harold Lloyd. Department stores molded storefront mannequins in his likeness.

Fujita designed his own flamboyant costumes to wear at glitzy parties or while bicycling around the town, managing to get mentioned frequently in gossip columns and fashion magazines. But he spent his fortune as fast as it came rolling in; Fujita gave his girlfriend Yuki an automobile with a bronze Rodin sculpture on the radiator cap.

While Fujita was clearly the top celebrity of the Japanese artists in Paris, there is evidence that Yasushi Tanaka was a second runner-up. In the art magazines and journals of the time, in lengthy reviews of European and American artists, I have found both "M. Foujita" and "M. Yasushi Tanaka" frequently mentioned side-by-side as contemporaries.

Salons and Cafes

WITHIN THE FIRST YEAR of his arrival, Yasushi wasted no time in getting his paintings admitted to two salons: *Salon d'Automne* and the *Salon de la Nationale*. Even so, Yasushi felt driven to expand himself beyond the academic salons where he risked being lost in the crowd. He managed to exhibit one-man shows at several art galleries by earning the patronage of art dealers such as Felix

Simonson of the *Galeries Simonson*, and by cultivating a network of friendships with European and American artists.

He earned glowing yet bittersweet reviews in magazines such as *American Art News* that managed both to compliment his talents while reinforcing his other-ness as an Asian. "Tanaka is a Japanese artist who, without repudiating those peculiar faculties for acute observation characteristic of his countrymen, has adapted them to the western form of painting, which he has very quickly assimilated. Our technique no doubt appeared to him as a means for expressing and rendering life more truthfully than that used by the Japanese masters and, though it afforded difficulties more arduous to overcome than those in the style which is obviously more natural to him, he assumed it without hesitation or compromise."

In Paris, he did not encounter the prudish conservatives that plagued him in Seattle. His nudes were well received and appreciated in a variety of publications, both in English and in French. *American Art News* described his portraits as excellent. "Tanaka's personality is emphasized in his nudes and large decorative compositions. Their supple design, unusual disposition, transparency of flesh tints and candor of their paganism gives them a charm quite apart. The title of one large painting: 'Nude Woman Standing by a Piano,' may sound dubious. In reality there is nothing equivocal about it, so free is it of suggestiveness. It seems quite natural that this beautiful woman should stand unrobed in her salon in the company of another, seated at a little distance, who is fully dressed. It is a very fine piece of work, free and direct, broadly handled, luminous and warm in color."

On the anniversary of their arrival, in June 1921, Yasushi penned a letter to Frederick Torrey to share the glowing news of his early successes. "Paris, I am glad to have been convinced, does certainly respond to art, and I am happy and immensely encouraged to think that my 11 years' hard work, the toil of [a] secluded sort, brought me here to the real place for art where, since my first appearance as a Salon d'Automne exhibitor, so much attention has been paid for my art." He also mentions the issue of his race and nationality affecting his public image, a hurdle that Caucasian artists were not challenged to overcome. His art could not be accepted purely on its merits but came to be viewed through a distorted lens seeking to psychoanalyze the artist based on his race. Yasushi writes, "Some critics declare that I am a painter of ardor and passion while the others think that I have been too much Americanized and my soul has gone out of my blood, etc. I am rather energized to find out that the French hardly understand the modern Japanese who are truly not the Orientals any longer."

In the same letter, Yasushi mentions his intent to visit his mother in Japan. Clearly, he is keeping up correspondence with his brothers. "I am expecting to go to Japan sometime next year just for a short visit to my old mother who has waited for me for seventeen years since I left her at the stage coach station now changed to the magnificent station of the electric car service. Several years ago, my brothers built a house for mother on the shore near Yokohama where one can see every steamer that comes in and goes out. There, my mother is to see my boat going in."

Yasushi also maintained contact with Yoshiatsu Shiota, an acquaintance from Seattle and an import/export merchant. Years before, Mr. Shiota had commissioned Yasushi to paint his portrait and purchased several of his wistful landscape paintings. After returning to Japan in the 1920s, Mr. Shiota tried, unsuccessfully, to arrange for an exhibition in Tokyo. He diligently saved a collection of their correspondence through the years that passed on to the archives of a modern museum in Japan.

The early years of the 1920s were Yasushi's most prolific period, when he produced numerous fresh paintings to add to his oeuvre of over a hundred paintings shipped over from his Seattle days. He exhibited often at prestigious salons and galleries side-by-side with the celebrated European artists of the day. A write-up in *The Paris Review* describes his work, "It disengages a penetrating modern spirit, discriminating and selective, ardent, intuitive, vigorous and refined." Another review in the French magazine *L'Avenir*, as quoted in *American Art News* says, "Yasushi Tanaka paints with the most delicate, most precise of sensibilities."

Yet, even in giving compliments, the reviewers make reference to his origins as if it were remarkable for an Asian to have artistic talents equal to his European peers. The *Journal du Peuple*, as quoted in *American Art News,* wrote, "Some of these landscapes evince quite extraordinary Western sensibility and altogether his work contradicts many a theory on the characteristic idiosyncrasies of races." Another issue of *American Art News* compares Yasushi to a well-known wood block print illustrator from the previous century. "It is a very arduous effort this Europeanized Oriental has to make of defying comparison with his antecedents, and it needed much courage. There is, of course, absolutely no reason why a Japanese should continue to draw forever like Hiroshige."

Meanwhile, as Yasushi basked in the thrill of producing new artworks, exhibiting his old work from the Seattle days, and immersing himself in the Paris art world, Louise devoted herself to rejuvenating her stagnant writing career. In those early years after their arrival in Paris, she contributed a number of articles to journals such as *The International Studio* that profiled contemporary French artists. Louise wrote insightful, scholarly critiques of J.L. Forain, Jean Marchand, and others. Her thoroughly researched article on Monticelli was intended as a precursor to a longer biography.

She caught the eye of *New York Times* reporter Merle Schuster visiting Paris in 1923. In an article titled, "Paris, the Literary Capital of the United States: French Atmosphere For American Writing," he describes the boatloads of Americans disembarking with mysterious black boxes containing portable typewriters carried to Paris by "the literary insurgents of America." The full-page article goes on to list several authors who spend their days at the well-known Café de Dome working their latest novels: Willa Cather, Edith Wharton, Edna St. Vincent Millay, Solita Solano, Janet Flanner of *The New Yorker* magazine, and the famous poets Ezra Pound and Gertrude Stein. Included farther down the list is "Louise Gebhard Cann, frequent contributor to the *International Studio*. Miss Cann may be seen at the *Bibliotheque Nationale* every day working on a 'Life of Monticelli' that promises to be the most important opus ever written about that artist. Having been accepted for publication upon completion by an English as well as an American house, there is already talk of a French translation."

Of course, the struggles of an unknown writer in Paris mirrored the struggles of a painter in the crowded over-saturated literary magazines and cafes of the Left Bank. I have not found any evidence that her longer biography of Monticelli, beyond a magazine article, was ever published. It appears that she did not continue to pursue fiction unlike her early years of short stories, poetry, and the one-act play. After moving to Paris, Louise focused solely on literary analysis in a written voice that calls to mind a university lecture.

In "The Present Literary Movement in France," published in *The Pacific Review*, under the byline of Louise Gebhard Cann, she describes the effect of World War I on contemporary French literature. "Some are written in a patriotic spirit with the heroic reactions, the romantic ideal of the soldier draping sorrow, horror, and tragedy... An astonishing amount of revolt against war, the conditions that lead up to it, its social results, is also voiced. I think no such frank writing would be permitted in America even now." By her critique of a number of contemporary French works of literature, and her mention of attending the dedication of Rodin's bust of Stendhal in the Luxembourg gardens, one has the sense that Louise settled comfortably in the Parisian art and literary scene.

While Yasushi's paintings were well received, compared to the conservative backlash he experienced in Seattle, the mere exhibition at galleries or salons did not always lead to sales. On the practical side, most of their funds went to tubes of oil paint, canvases, framing costs, and photographers to catalog the finished product. All that a writer needs is a typewriter with paper and ink. They struggled in those early years for enough money to buy food and pay for the rent and heat on their apartment studio.

A series of personal letters from Louise to the Arctic explorer Vilhjalmur Stefansson tell the true story behind the glitz of favorable critic reviews and the series of flashy art exhibitions. Louise asked him for a personal loan and for referral to a publishing house, as Stefansson had successfully published accounts of his Arctic adventures. She described the realities of their situation: that studio space was expensive, that exhibitions in the salons were not profitable in the short-term, and her painstakingly researched articles paid only upon publication. Thus, in between wealthy patrons making purchases of paintings, and articles being accepted by journals or magazines, they had long periods of scraping for every franc. "In order to get [a better studio], we are obliged to pay rent in advance, three months at least, and to place in the bank a sum of money 3,500 francs to guarantee the rent. No landlord will make better terms than that here, and unless we can satisfy those exactions, we shall be unable to get a studio, for studios are most difficult to procure."

James Joyce

DURING THEIR ROCKY early years in Paris, the Tanakas became acquainted with the Irish novelist James Joyce, a modernist who wrote in a unique experimental style of prose. He is best known for "Portrait of the Artist as a Young Man," "Ulysses" and "Finnegan's Wake." Born in Dublin in 1882, roughly the same age as Louise and Yasushi, the author spent most of his adulthood as an itinerant traveling around Europe. He shared a romantic partnership with Nora Barnacle for over twenty years but would not legally marry her until 1931. The couple had two children, Giorgio and Lucia, while they lived in Italy before moving to Paris in the early 1920s.

Joyce's notoriety preceded him for several years. Advance chapters of his novel-in-progress "Ulysses" had been published in serial installments in *The Little Review* literary journal. As a side note, the controversial novel "Ulysses" would have never seen the light of day if not for the direct support of Sylvia Beach, the owner of the Paris bookstore Shakespeare & Co., who made the risky financial and professional investment in him. Sylvia Beach's small press did the first publication of Ulysses in 1922 when no one else would touch this controversial material due to a loud outcry of obscenity. Even after it was printed, the book was widely banned. Customs inspectors routinely seized copies by the boxload and burned them on the docks.

The Tanakas met James Joyce in a roundabout way. Louise boldy wrote a letter to the poet Ezra Pound, who was then living in Paris and was known to be a patron of artists with an interest in Japanese artists particularly. It appears that Pound did not accommodate her request to help Yasushi get an exhibition, most likely because Pound had already taken another Japanese painter, Tamijuro Kume, under his wing.

Instead, Ezra Pound recommended Louise to James Joyce himself. Both men shared an interest in all things Japanese going back at least a decade to their days in London when Pound was commissioned by the widow of Ernest Fenollosa in 1912 to polish and prepare for publication Fenollosa's translation of classical Japanese Noh plays.

Joyce, as well as Pound, collected art books and had a special fascination of Japanese poetry. He was certainly aware of the Japanese poet Yone Noguchi living in London, which brings the "small world" element around to Yasushi's association with Joaquin Miller's sanctuary in California. Joyce's journals show a familiarity with aspects of Japan's complex written language and a fascination with the idea of depicting words in pictorial form rather than spelling with the alphabet. Joyce's work is notorious for inventing words of Japanese origin, and conversely his works were in high demand to be translated into Japanese. The translation of his novel "Ulysses" in two volumes from Daiichi Shobo Press appeared in the early 1930s.

Joyce visited the Tanakas a few days before the end of the year 1920, in answer to Louise's letter. Joyce felt refreshed to speak English as he had just come from several years of living in Italy, and worried that by speaking Italian he was losing his English. Louise was already a Joyce fan, as an avid reader of modern literature and a long-time subscriber to *The Little Review*.

Louise recalled in her first meeting with Joyce, that he expressed disdain for most works of art except portraiture. Aside from being at odds on that issue, as both she and Yasushi felt disdain for portraiture, she described him as very pleasant and agreeable. He spoke of his time in Italy, his interest in Homer, and wore his erudition very naturally. Joyce lent her a manuscript of Ulysses and some clippings for her reference. She did write the article but could never succeed in getting it published.

Years later, in 1954, a fellow named Richard Ellman was writing a biography of James Joyce, and he traveled to Paris for research. He corresponded with Louise—still living in the same apartment—and met with her to discuss her recollections. Copies of their letters and Ellman's notes on the interviews are kept in university archives. His notes offer clues that Louise Cann (a.k.a. Mrs. Tanaka) was a congenial, gracious hostess when visitors came to call. In the conversations with Mr. Ellman, Louise described their cafe-esque acquaintance, sharing anecdotes such as the time when Louise said to Nora, "You are a martyr to a man of genius," and Nora had laughingly agreed.

On the social side, Joyce introduced them to Vouvray wine that he always drank after dinner. Joyce was working every day on his writing and used to go out in the evenings although, at parties, he hardly said a word. The cafe Dome was their primary daytime rendezvous. One of their preferred evening venues was the Bal Bullier dance hall, a grand popular establishment opposite the statue of Marshal Ney described by Hemingway in his memoirs "A Moveable Feast." At the Bal Bullier, they all danced to the lively piano music, except for

Joyce who preferred to sing. Joyce stayed out very late—too late for the Tanakas who preferred to retire earlier.

According to Louise, Joyce was faithfully devoted to Nora and stressed that she was his only true love. Nora had suffered from poverty in her youth, and so she loved dressing and living well. Louise also told Mr. Ellman that Joyce's daughter Lucia was very beautiful. She would have been 18 years old in 1925 and attended dance school. According to Louise, Yasushi thought her one of the most beautiful girls he had ever seen—a cast in her eye added to her distinctiveness. These anecdotes were told to Mr. Ellman years later, when it became well known that Lucia struggled with severe mental illness and was institutionalized for the remainder of her adult life.

Following Mr. Ellman's interview in the 1950s, Louise wrote a letter of thanks for his gift of an article, "The Backgrounds of Ulysses," that she read with keen interest. In the letter, Louise shares that she had only read "Ulysses" in manuscript, never in the final published form. She knew of the literary allusions to Queen Victoria, for example, concealed in metaphor, only from her personal conversations with Joyce himself. She also gave her opinion of being concerned for the posthumous legacy of so-called "great men." One has to wonder if she meant not only Joyce or Pound but her own husband. Saying to Nora Joyce that she was a "martyr to a man of genius," she may have been speaking of herself. "What will happen next in the lives of great men? ...There's a great difference between meeting a person, visiting with him or her, and all that inner dimension which is the hinterland of the real personality.... There's something almost oriental about Joyce. A Japanese artist or poet can make even a piece of string, or an old bent nail significant. All was grist to his mill. I didn't see the old bent nail or the string in the Retrospective, though they were probably there, since for him everything he came in contact with had meaning."

Ezra Pound's Apartment

AFTER TWO YEARS OF gaining a foothold in the Parisian art and literature scene, the Tanakas made plans to relocate back to Japan for at least a year. Their plans changed when Yasushi's mother suddenly passed away. Yasushi wrote in a letter to Frederick Torrey, on Oct. 28, 1922, "My wife and I were planning to visit Japan for at least a year or so mainly for holding my exhibitions at Tokyo. I had received many letters from my brothers urging us to go there to see my old mother who had a great hope in my temperament but who became almost impatient of writing for my return. I have stayed out for eighteen years. And I finally made up my mind to visit my old Japan, which has become newer and newer since my departure, and see my old mother who had become dreadfully old since my farewell to her. But Alas!—too late, my poor mother died when we were just getting ready to pack our trunks! As a boy of thirteen I used to read the Chinese formula for piety: 'The trees waited to be calm, but the wind never ceases; the child is eager to take care of the parents, but the old ones never wait.' We were entirely discouraged. "

They unpacked their steamer trunks and remained in Paris, at 3 Villa Brune, Paris 14e, to continue pursuing their goals as artist and writer. Oddly, they did not follow through on a trip to Japan even to attend his mother's funeral. As far as I know, Yasushi never saw his brothers again.

In the same letter, Yasushi informs Torrey that his one-man show at the Galerie de Marsan was a success and he sold a painting. He also shares news of Louise's writing career with her critique articles soon to be published in art journals such as *L'Art de les Artistes* and *International Studio*. He describes the mood of Paris in somewhat gloomy terms. "After the war, even the climate of Paris must have changed; people are strangely tormented, naturally they feel more dreary. Now in Paris comfort is very expensive.... We hear art in America is in New York thriving. Paris, for the present, is still bad, worse than during the war yet."

By the summer of 1923, the Tanakas' fortune had not yet risen beyond the perpetual worry of making ends meet from day to day. They moved from 3 Villa Brune, 14e to an apartment at 72 bis Rue Notre Dame des Champs, 6e. With only six months left on the lease, they felt the squeeze of a relentless housing crisis as they searched again for a new home.

The American expatriate poet, Ezra Pound had come to Paris with his wife Dorothy in January 1921. He took up residence at 70 bis Rue Notre-Dame-des-Champs, next door to apartment 72 bis where the Tanakas would come to stay two years later. Aside from writing poems, he spent most of his time building furniture for his apartment and shelves for the bookstore Shakespeare and Company—a core fixture of the Paris literary scene.

Ezra Pound is a controversial figure, on the one hand a brilliant poet who helped to reshape the modern literary world. He served as a mentor and icon to star authors of the early 20th century. It is widely recognized that many careers would have withered into obscurity without Ezra Pound's direct support, such as William Butler Yeats, James Joyce, Ernest Hemingway, or Robert Frost. He critiqued and edited their early drafts manuscripts. He compiled anthologies of their works, introduced them to publishers, and arranged to get their novels into bookstores. In the lean times, he also donated money or clothes.

On the other hand, during World War II, he became a celebrity supporter of the fascist dictator Mousselini. Shortly before Hitler's army took over the city of Paris, Ezra Pound relocated to Italy where he made over a hundred radio broadcasts. His enraged, paranoid rantings survive in transcripts or audio recordings so there is no doubt that he passionately amplified anti-Semitic conspiracy theories that Jewish bankers operated in a shadowy cabal to control the world's finances.

Hemingway spearheaded the efforts, after World War II, to rehabilitate his old friend's reputation by declaring that Ezra Pound must have gone insane. Surely, only an insane person could have supported the horrors of the Nazi holocaust. Louise appears to have jumped aboard Hemingway's he-must-be-pitied-not-shunned bandwagon. She published an article in 1955 for the *Pound Newsletter*, in commemoration of the poet's 70th birthday. She sidesteps any mention of Pound's notoriety and instead describes at length how she had been a follower of his earlier writings, and how they were lucky to win occupancy of the coveted apartment.

In describing her early fangirl days, she writes, "Before coming to France, I had followed his articles in *The Little Review*, delighted with his iconoclasm, for American literature had become so anemic that even the general reader was beginning to hanker after at least a modicum of vigor and a more realistic presentation of-the way of the world. At the close of World War I, we were still suffering from a mid-Victorian hang-over. Insipid superficiality, to say nothing of hypocrisy, failed to coordinate the experience of life with the fruitful soil which is the basis of literature. Ibsen had set up a ferment of freedom of individual expression and self-fulfillment. Personal revolts were the powder that finally Ezra Pound ignited. He fought and drove a wedge into the barrier maintained by a senile authority that feared and suppressed frank speaking. A group of us out West, among them university students, met in our studio and read and discussed everything of his we could lay hands on. We submitted gleefully to the frowns our quotations provoked. We gloried in him, though we hardly realized what radical and liberating changes his sarcasms and sneers and his example would-bring about. With his combative genius, he released in the up-coming generation a creative force, smoldering under a lid, with the result that American novels and poetry have exerted and are more and more exerting, worldwide influence."

The circumstances of winning the soon-to-be-vacated apartment were a mixture of luck and the cultivating of relationships with the building's concierge. "It was in the summer of 1923, when we were living at 72, Rue N.D. des Champs, that a student from Columbia University came to see us and said she'd just been at a cocktail party given by Ezra Pound in his studio which was in a garden next door. At 70 bis, a long passageway flanked by ivied stone walls lead from the street to the garden, the trees of which could be seen from the outer gate.... About the beginning of September, I believe, our conciérge, sister-in-law of the conciérge next door, came up and informed us that a studio with a room or two attached was available, because the occupant, Mr. Pound, was giving it up."

This word, concierge, has a unique tradition in the city of Paris. From about the mid-19th century, with the rise of apartment building clusters with multiple doorways, a gatekeeper became necessary to manage the potential chaos of owners, renters, and servants. The concierge usually lived in ground floor rooms that offered a view of comings-and-goings. The concierge kept keys to all the apartments, handled mail, screened visitors, and acted as counselor or nanny to wayward children. Most importantly, they formed a network of concierges among all the apartment buildings and kept up with the happenings around the city. When police went in search of someone, their first visit was to the concierge.

Louise explains, "We lived in a furnished lodging that had to be given up within six months and the time was running out. We had been frantically seeking for a foothold on which we could get a lease so we could continue with our work but everything we looked at was tied up with a big premium....

Madame Davaze, the conciérge at 70 bis was a stout, heavy woman. She conducted us to the appointment with the poet. On entering, she edged over to the side of the door laughing. The floor sagged in the middle. She kept on the rim of what looked as if it would soon be a hole.... A bay, its three sides and roof of glass, projected into the garden and formed the north side of the apartment, with the exception of tall windows that sprang from a beam which divides the verandah, as we call it, from the studio."

Of Ezra Pound himself, Louise gives her impression of meeting him for the first time. Her words are chosen carefully to offer an apologetic image of the man who had become an international pariah at the time of her writing this article. She emphasizes his gentle demeanor and his courteous manners. She compares him to a high school teacher. "There was an engaging simplicity in his manner of greeting us, an uninhibited affability. No pose, no intimidating reserve—-just a pleasant person according us the opportunity to take over the living and working place we so agonizingly needed and facilitating the transaction.... His appearance and manner were not what I had expected. One could hardly imagine this smiling young man ridiculing Tennyson, or blasting popular magazines, or indulging in a crusade. Nothing harsh or colorful accented his speech. His voice, rather thin, had none of the metallic clang of his poems and satires."

In hindsight, but for her knowledge of Pound's early writings and her brief, cordial encounters, Louise did not truly know the man. She held to the romantic notion of the writer's voice she had known in her college days—perhaps at Cornell, when she was the miserable wife of a mathematics professor or when she was shunned by her family for creating public scandals of her own. Indeed, it would be necessary for her to engage in cognitive dissonance, to disregard Pound's fascist tirades as the ravings of a madman, to maintain her idolized image of the man she imagined him to be in her youth rather than the man he truly was.

Louise reveals her sentimentality in this passage, from her article in the Pound Newsletter, where she mentions a huge Godin cast iron stove that loomed on a dividing strip of stone. "Mr. Pound put his hand [on it] with a gesture of *estime*, saying, 'It's old. Was here when we came, but I assure you it heats.' And so it did, until after the war, when one day it broke out with something that looked like smallpox and refused to burn. Mr. Pound had left it to us as a legacy so when I had the poor old thing removed, being a sentimental person, I felt as if I'd closed an era."

A rare painting best represents this period in Yasushi's life. The theme is perhaps borrowed from a classic titled "The Artist's Studio" painted by Gustave Courbet in the mid-1850s. Fujita the genius of self-marketing has a number of photographs and portraits of himself at work in his studio. Yasushi—as Fujita's nearest competitor—also has one of these scenes committed to canvas. Apparently unsigned, the work could be the product of Yasushi's own hand, or one of his students, or a colleague in his circle of acquaintances. According to the website Artnet, this painting sold at private auction to a private collector.

The setting is clearly the apartment formerly occupied by Ezra Pound, showing the conservatory area's the large windows and hints of trees and chimneys outdoors. One of Yasushi's framed paintings of a nude is represented in miniature. Other paintings are cluttered in the background, draped in cloths. On the left side stands a nude model. At her feet sits another model partially draped in a veil. A third woman with a fur-edged velvet robe is conversing with a bald, bespectacled man smoking a cigar in the background. Apparently, the man is a prospective buyer or an art collector.

On the right, Yasushi is seated before a large canvas on an easel—the back side of the canvas facing the viewer—and he is intently studying the nude model who stands nearby. His hand rests on his thigh holding his paintbrush at the ready. Just behind Yasushi, a woman who resembles Louise sits either on the floor or a low stool. She holds an open book cradled in her lap but she is not focused on her book at the moment. Her hand drapes down to brush the floor and her eyes, through spectacles, gaze downward.

Japan in Turmoil

YASUSHI'S SIBLINGS in Japan experienced a major earthquake on Saturday, September 1, 1923. The disaster utterly devastated the capital city of Tokyo, the bustling port city of Yokohama, and caused widespread damage throughout the surrounding prefectures. Estimated casualties totaled more than 100,000 deaths, and roughly two million people lost their homes.

The disaster struck at midday when many people were cooking lunch. A strong typhoon blowing from offshore brought high winds to Tokyo Bay. The gas pipes and cooking fires escalated into a fire tornado that killed a greater number of people than the earthquake alone. Water pipes[1] broke all over the city, impeding the ability to extinguish the fires quickly. If that weren't enough, a tsunami with waves as high as 10 meters (33 feet) struck the coast and caused even more death and destruction.

Japan was shaken to the core of its soul. This natural disaster caused widespread death, homelessness, and economic hardships. Nationalistic, anti-foreigner sentiments fueled racist mob violence against ethnic Koreans who had lived in Japan for generations but who still faced severe discrimination. The national ideology turned to the extreme, beginning a trajectory that would have consequences over the next several decades for Japan and the world.

Living in Paris, far away from the tragedy, Yasushi only heard about the events in his hometown from newspapers. He kept up correspondence with his brothers, who all survived the earthquake, but one has to wonder how much all those years away from home pursuing his art career eroded his relationship with his family.

He had not seen his brothers since he left home at age eighteen. Now as a man in his late thirties, and his mother having already passed away, the desire to return to his native country was fading. Did his brothers harbor resentment for Yasushi not returning for his mother's funeral, not assisting the family after the earthquake, and for remaining in a foreign land to pursue his own ambitions? Japanese culture places a high premium on the individual's subservience to the group, the maintaining of group harmony at all costs; by staying in Paris to seek his fame and fortune, Yasushi was bucking the system. I doubt that his brothers could ever fully understand that painting was his life, his soul, his reason for existence, and nowhere else but Paris could he achieve his dreams.

Yasushi wrote a letter to the art dealer Frederick Torrey five months after the earthquake. He candidly reveals a mixture of emotions, that his brothers and his collection of paintings have almost equal weight in his mind. "My wife and I were in a terrible anxiety to know what has become of my three younger brothers at Yokohama and several important paintings of mine that had just

1. https://en.wikipedia.org/wiki/Water_mains

arrived in Japan for sale and for exhibit. However, soon afterwards we learned from my older brother of the safety of all my younger brothers and from my friend in Tokyo of that of all my paintings. Although I lost the chance for realizing over thousand dollars from the pictures I had sent, my wife and I were quite relieved as to know how miraculous it was that all my brothers and their families were unharmed by the disaster." In this letter, he excitedly shares with Torrey the news that one of his paintings was chosen to hang in the prestigious Luxembourg museum, and another was purchased for the *Musee de Tokyo* (the Matsukata Museum) where it remains to this day. "I am now selling my nudes at my own prices which two years ago were considered by the French almost fantastic. My nudes are also keenly coveted by various Italian, Spanish, and German collectors."

In this letter to Torrey, in 1924, Yasushi also mentions the two Japanese princes Higashikuni and Asaka who attended his exhibit and who graciously received him and Louise. Yasushi must have felt euphoric to converse with imperial family members face-to-face while his father would have prostrated face-down on the floor. Until the 20th century it was unthinkable for an ordinary citizen to carry on a conversation with someone of such an exalted class. The Emperor and the royal family rarely made public appearances and, even then, at a distance.

Paris in the 1920s created an oasis for free-thinking intellectuals and artists, where all the traditions of the past could be challenged or discarded with impunity. Yasushi describes how the imperial princes visited his exhibition. "They received my wife and myself in an extraordinary Occidental and democratic manner, and each purchased four paintings. It has been rumored that one of the important pieces may be presented to the Prince Regent at Tokyo, but this is kept discreet for the present, which I don't quite understand. The most curious fact is that the paintings their Highnesses have chosen are all nudes, the most conspicuous Tanaka nudes. The History of the Acquisition of Occidental nude paintings by the Royal family of Japan date from the days of my 1924 exhibition."

Japan's Prince Regent at the time would become the Emperor Hirohito just two years later. A shy, bookish fellow, he would be the titular emperor throughout the period of rising Japanese nationalism, militarism, and aggression into Manchuria. Likewise, the princes Higashikuni and Asaka may have been fun party companions and gracious hosts in Paris, but their future life stories tell a darker side.

Prince Naruhiko Higashikuni was a career officer in the Imperial Japanese Army who went to Paris from 1920 to 1926 to learn military tactics at the universities. Roughly a decade later, Higashikuni would become a general in the Imperial Japanese army that invaded Manchuria in the 1930s and he personally authorized brutal tactics such as the use of poison gas on civilians. His half-brother Prince Asaka would become the commander of Japanese military forces outside the Chinese city of Nanking. When the army made its final assault to capture the city, Prince Asaka issued the order to kill all captives and take no prisoners—the wholesale massacre of thousands.

Returning now to their youthful misadventures in Paris, the princes engaged in playboy behavior that caused numerous public scandals. Higashikuni openly consorted with a French mistress. He enjoyed high living and fast cars, of which Europe had the best. An automobile accident caused the death of another royal cousin and gave Asaka a lifelong limp. Yet the band played on. The great Kanto earthquake of 1923, and the death of one of his sons, was not enough to lure Higashikuni back to the homeland where his wife waited under the cloud of public embarrassment. Eventually the Imperial Household Ministry would dispatch a chamberlain to Paris to force Higashikuni to return home.

One wonders how much of the princes' extravagant lifestyle rubbed off on Yasushi, who was roughly their same age. Perhaps it was the decadent culture of Paris itself. The mid-1920s appears to mark the beginning of his professional decline. Yasushi found that more overtly erotic paintings were in demand by foreign collectors. In other words, eroticism paid the bills. He produced more and more depictions of nudes in salacious poses—no longer posed sweetly behind silk veils or as abstract shapes of light flesh against darker backgrounds. Inevitably, Yasushi crossed the line and began carrying on casual affairs with his models. One particular redhead appears frequently in Yasushi's nude scenes. Even so, Yasushi and Louise held their marriage together through the wild times of Paris in the 1920s. By contrast, Monsieur Foujita carried on a so-called open marriage for several years before he divorced to marry his favorite model Lucie a.k.a. Yuki.

As the decade wore on, the Asian artists in Paris continued to experience barriers to their success compared to their European or American peers. Hundreds of Japanese artists living in Paris resorted to organizing their own exhibition in June 1926, at the Galerie Zivy near the Champs-Elysees. The Japanese ambassador to France and the French Minister of education and art attended the gala event of 145 works by more than fifty artists, including Yasushi Tanaka.

Despite favorable reviews, it does not appear that the Japanese exhibition gained momentum. A few years later, in October 1929, the Roaring Twenties went out with a bang when the stock market crashed and plunged the world into the worst economic depression of the 20th century.

Surviving the Thirties

FOR THE EARLY YEARS of the 1930s, there was a lingering hope that the Great Depression would not be as bad as it turned out to be. Several waves of financial panics over the past fifty years gave the impression, at first, that the world economy cycled through dips and recoveries. The art and literary community of Paris, in particular, carried on much as before.

A curiously light-hearted piece appeared in Louise's hometown newspaper the *Seattle Sunday Times*, April 6, 1930. In "Tanaka, Former Seattle Artist, Triumphs Abroad" the reporter Stanley Orne celebrates Yasushi's successes but also paints him as an eccentric character inhabiting the cafes of Paris. The fact that he is mistaken for the silent film star Charlie Chaplin gives a clue at his public image, a shabby wardrobe and unkempt thick hair, in stark contrast to the neatly-trimmed bowl cut of Monsieur Foujita.

> American visitors to Montparnasse, the new Latin quarter of Paris, vow that Charlie Chaplin is a habitué of the students' and artists' district.
>
> "No, that's not Charlie Chaplin," the old residents inform inquirers. "That's Yusushi [sic] Tanaka, a Japanese artist. But he does resemble

> Chaplin. His American wife thinks they look so much alike that she calls him C.C."
>
> This tabloid question-answer drama takes place nearly every time the Seattle-reared Japanese husband of a Seattle American woman, leaves his studio. It happens most often at the Coupole, an immense international restaurant which somewhat outshines the glamour of the older, smaller, more famous Dome, Select, and Rotonde cafes on the Boulevard Montparnasse.
>
> Tanaka may be sitting with friends in the Coupole, reproducing facially the expressions of each person who passes along the aisle. Some say that his pantomimic powers are funnier than Chaplin's. Because of this talent newcomers to Montparnasse are doubly sure that they are seeing Chaplin.
>
> "Isn't that Charlie Chaplin over there?" they whisper into someone's ear.
>
> "No, that's Tanaka, the Japanese artist," someone replies. "He's an odd sort. One night he rushed half-dressed out into the chilly night, accosted a policeman, handed him 50 francs, and then ran on after catching a fleeting glimpse of the flat-foot's face. He painted from memory a picture of the policeman's puzzled face."

Meanwhile, Louise found her true calling as a scholarly critic of the modern art movement in Paris. She joined the American Women's Club, founded in 1921 as a social and educational outlet for English-speaking women of all nations who found themselves living as "ex-pats" in Paris. Louise was an active member during the 1930s, as a regular lecturer on topics of modern art in the monthly meetings, as documented and reproduced in the club's monthly Bulletin.

Louise developed and maintained a friendship with Janet Flanner, a columnist who wrote the series "Letters from Paris" for *The New Yorker* magazine under the pen name Genet. The articles are a valuable contemporary journal of changes taking place in the city over the years. However, the only hard evidence of their friendship is Yasushi's oil portrait of Janet Flanner's long-time companion, the novelist Solita Solano.

She continued to find publishing success in biographies—profiles and analysis of contemporary artists—that are scattered in the holdings of various libraries to this day. Her only full-length book appears to be a biography of the Post-Impressionist painter Pierre Laprade, co-authored with input from the artist himself, published in 1930 the year before his death. Her other published title is an illustrated, staple-bound booklet for the retrospective exposition at the Galerie Jean Charpentier, in 1937, to commemorate and analyze the paintings of the late Eugene Lawrence Vail.

At least for the early part of the decade, his name still carried weight. He is the only other Japanese artist mentioned—along with the famous Fujita—in a 1932 issue of *The Brooklyn Museum Quarterly* describing generous gifts from their collection of two patrons. Among the European artists were listed "...two studies of the human figure by Yasushi Tanaka and Foujita, both having a high reputation for their painting in the western manner and yet piquantly suggesting the Japanese element in their work."

It appears that Yasushi's production of artwork declined in the mid-1930s, although his output from year to year is difficult to assess. Neither he nor Louise kept an accurate catalog of his works, of what they shipped from Seattle or New York, what he sent to Japan before the great earthquake of 1923, or what he produced while in Paris. He did not label his canvases with a title or date, and generally neglected to sign them. An inventory of his *oeuvre* (the artist's body of work) can be reconstructed, partially at best, only from the scraps of exhibition brochures or photo reproductions in published articles.

His paintings of nude women became more overtly erotic, riding the wave of contemporary social trends. After all, it was in 1934 that Henry Miller released his novel "Tropic of Cancer" through a publisher in Paris—a book that was quickly banned in the United States for its very explicit descriptions of the protagonist's sexual exploits. Yet even in his erotic subject matter, Yasushi is not as bold or experimental as he could have been. He maintains a sense of tradition by paying homage to classics in at least two pieces, described below.

Leda and the Swan. The subject matter is based on a classical Greek myth, where the god Zeus transformed into a swan and descended to Earth to seduce a woman named Leda. The motif appears in antiquity and the Middle Ages but in the Italian Renaissance it gained renewed popularity. Many well-known artists over the years, from Michelangelo to Cezanne, have done some version of illustrating this myth to varying degrees of eroticism.

Yasushi's rendition portrays Leda as whole-heartedly embracing the swan in a passionate grip, her cheeks flushed pink, her eyes shut. There is no question that the experience is consensual and mutually pleasurable. The swan is wildly flapping his wings and loose feathers are flying everywhere. Overall the mood is one of chaotic abandon.

Nude Woman Having A Dream. The misshapen monster embracing a sleeping woman from behind, one claw-like hand groping her naked breast, is most likely an interpretation of Henry Fuseli's "The Nightmare" (1781) that depicted a demon perched on the chest of a sleeping woman. An incubus is a male demon who tempts women into illicit sexual activity, usually while they are sleeping. The Fuseli painting was well known in its day, copied in etchings and reproduced. There are allusions to this painting in the works of 19th century horror authors Edgar Allen Poe and Mary Shelley.

Yasushi's version on this theme enlarges the incubus to human size. Instead of sitting on the woman's chest, he embraces her from behind. The background is a floral print of some kind, suggesting a decorative rug or sofa. The sleeping woman's expression is serene and her left hand unconsciously drapes over the monster's head, bringing his featureless sloth face closer to her neck. Again, there is no question that the experience is consensual and mutually pleasurable. Also, like the scattered feathers of Leda and the Swan, there are splotches of shadows across the nude's body that are the same tones as the monster's skin. The two figures are blended in a union of color and form.

The worldwide economy did not rebound by the mid-1930s, as many had hoped, and the Great Depression cast a shadow over everything. The market for luxury items, especially the fine arts, fell off sharply. Wealthy art collectors with cash flowing out their pockets disappeared. Yasushi's community of expats also dwindled beginning with his most prestigious patrons, the Japanese princes, who resumed their roles in the imperial family. Monsieur Foujita embarked for South America to avoid paying French taxes on his luxury automobiles and the profits of his artistic endeavors. As the support of salons and patrons evaporated, the hundreds of Japanese aspiring artists abandoned their Paris ambitions and returned to their homeland.

As he had done back in Seattle, when bills needed to be paid, Yasushi turned to teaching art students. He mentions a few in his correspondence with Frederick Torrey, and he maintains a cordial professional relationship with Mr. Guzman and Mr. Butler formerly of the Seattle Fine Arts Association.

One of Yasushi's notable success stories, that I discovered, was an American sculptor named Frederick Charles Shrady. Born in New York, his father was also a sculptor of public statues, most notably the Grant Memorial in honor of President Ulysses S. Grant displayed on the grounds of the U.S. capitol. Today, Frederick Shrady is best known for his statues installed at prominent landmarks, to name only a few: "Peter, Fisher of Men" at Fordham University's campus; a bronze figure of the American-born Roman Catholic saint Mother Elizabeth Seton at St. Patrick's Cathedral; and, a marble statue of "Our Lady of Fatima" commissioned by Pope John Paul II for the Vatican.

Frederick Shrady studied at a couple of schools before he moved to Paris with intent to pursue painting. He lived in Paris from 1931 to 1939, studying how to paint under Yasushi Tanaka's tutelage. From what I can see, Yasushi's influence is apparent in Shrady's technique and style. What he learned of painting, he carried into his later sculptures. As articulated by a contemporary critique : "...his powerful sense of the dramatic gesture to express an act or idea is always given to us through interplays or extreme tension between the flowing elements of his design. The parts seem to strive against each other in sweeping lines of almost choreographed gestures—and then to come together in the whole to effect a great act of release. Ever so many of his works carry the effect of aspiration—rising like flame, a reaching in desire for that which can be attained only through the manifestation of the invisible."

At the 1937 Paris Exposition, Yasushi's student Frederick Shrady entered a painting and was awarded a medal. The International Exposition originally was conceived as an art expo in a long line of world's fair expositions that had gone before. The committee reconsidered the current dour mood of the world and expanded upon the theme. Decorative arts alone did not seem worthy of a large investment of labor and capital; science and industry rose to prominence in the public mind. The French restructured the event as an "Exposition of Decorative Arts and Modern Industry," adding exhibits of scientific and technological innovations along with the arts.

An older museum building was demolished and the new Chaillot Palace was constructed in its place. This new facility would also replace the Musée du Luxembourg that closed its doors this same year. The most notable fine art piece to debut at the expo was Picasso's "Guernica," an strikingly heart-breaking portrayal of a recent military atrocity in northern Spain perpetrated by Nazi Germany and Italian fascists.

A number of countries erected pavilions that showcased their national identities—France, Italy, Japan, Spain, the United States, etc. The striking pavilions of Nazi Germany and the Soviet Union were positioned to face off against each other. In the most memorable souvenir photographs of the cityscape, the two towers with their opposing emblems face off at either side of the Eiffel Tower. Larger-than-life statues crowned each tower: "Facing the heroically posed Russian workingman and peasant woman brandishing hammer and sickle, the German eagle, its talons clutching a wreath encircling a huge swastika, disdainfully turned its head and fanned out its wings. At the ground level, a massively naked Teutonic trio stares at the Russian monument with grim determination." The gates closed on the Exposition in November 1937, and the respective nations packed up and went home to their own shores.

Circumstances in Paris grew dire as the 1930s wore on into the second half of the decade. All of Europe worked to build up its war machine, and Japan built up its national military on the pretext of defending Asia from the incursion of European colonization. Germany and Japan became uneasy allies with the signing of the Anti-Comintern Pact of 1936, ostensibly in opposition to the spread of communism from the Soviet Union and Russia's ally China.

As Charlie Chaplin himself would say in one of his later films, with sound, "In this world there is room for everyone, and the good earth is rich and can provide for everyone. The way of life can be free and beautiful, but we have lost the way. Greed has poisoned men's souls, has barricaded the world with hate, has goose-stepped us into misery and bloodshed."

Yasushi and Louise remained sheltered in the bubble of the Parisian art and literature community. Louise gave a lecture to the American Women's Club, on February 16, 1936, titled "Art and Nature" that discussed her husband's style of art. I have no information of what Yasushi may have learned from afar of his country's military aggression, the invasion of Manchuria, if he received Japanese-language newspapers, or if he received correspondence from friends or family living in Japan. Louise by then had no family ties in the United States—her parents and siblings all had passed away. She was fully assimilated to Parisian life. It appears likely that the Tanakas both occupied their minds with beautiful things while, all around them, the world descended into brutality and greedy empires expanded beyond their borders.

Meanwhile, back in the U.S., Yasushi's old friend "Issio" Kuge reverted fully to his original name of Ichizo and no longer associated with poets and artists. In the 1930s, he settled into a comfortably steady position as the head waiter at Woodway Country Club in picturesque Darien, Connecticut, not far from the shoreline that faces New York's Long Island. City directories show that he stayed in the same place throughout the Great Depression years. Ironically, he established himself in the type of service role that Charles Warren Stoddard had wished for: "He should bring me my mail or any daily papers... make my bed and me comfortable, and cook. Yes, to make it perfect... cook!" The last trace of Ichizo Kuge is the 1940 federal census, at age 59, where he continues to reside at Woodway Country Club and works in the restaurant at this exclusive golf resort. One has to wonder whatever happened to him in the years to follow.

By the time Hitler's army invaded Poland in September 1939, many of Yasushi's artist colleagues had already returned either to their homes in Japan or to their former lives in America. The lavish parties reminiscent of the Great Gatsby had long ceased, as had the salon exhibitions without wealthy art connoisseurs and patrons to foot the bills. Yasushi continued to teach students. Louise continued to lecture art theory and publish articles, but one can imagine their lives became more of a struggle in those lean years.

Paris in 1940

ON JUNE 14, 1940 THE German army rolled into Paris unopposed. The Vichy government of France surrendered to avoid bloodshed or utter destruction. Their top leaders were veterans of World War I and still remembered the horrible carnage, the losses in the millions. As the Nazi tanks rolled toward Paris, the art community evacuated from the Louvre Museum as much as they could. Precious classical art was shipped into the countryside to be hidden in farm houses and barns; anything to keep the treasures from falling into the greedy hands of Nazi art collectors.

It was a push by the twisted genius of propaganda, Joseph Goebbels, that the city's brothels, cabarets, cafes and restaurants should remain open for business. He wanted to give the illusion that Nazi forces were beneficent conquerors, that the social life of Parisiennes should not change, that the people should feel welcoming to their conquerors. It was called a bloodless surrender. The chilling casual presence of Nazi soldiers was enough to quell active resistance.

Yasushi and Louise saw it all: when Nazi uniforms strolled the streets and sat in sidewalk cafes where poets and artists used to sit. Crimson flags with the swastika symbol hung everywhere. The Nazis took control of all forms of media: the newspapers, the radio, cinema and literature. Censorship was absolute. Anything remotely critical of Germany, the Third Reich, or the occupation never saw the light of day. The residents of Paris risked arrest if they were caught listening to BBC radio broadcasts from England. In later years, the philosopher Sartre remarked, "During the occupation, we had two choices: collaborate or resist." Those who made the choice to do neither had a third option: to flee.

Gertrude Stein and her companion Alice B. Toklas, both Jews, had spent the summer of 1939 at their country home in a village east of Lyon. When the Nazi army invaded Poland, they made a quick trip to Paris, staying just long enough to collect essential belongings—and a couple of works by Cezanne and Picasso—but they did not return to the capital until after its liberation.

James Joyce in 1940 was already in ill health when he fled Paris ahead of the Germans. He was detained by immigration authorities in eastern France for several months before being allowed to enter Switzerland. When he finally reached Zurich, he died in January 1941 after undergoing surgery for a perforated ulcer.

Picasso remained in Paris throughout the occupation, in his studio on the rue des Grands-Augustins. It was there that an apocryphal exchange took place. Once a German officer, when offered a postcard reprint of the Guernica painting, turned angrily to Picasso and asked, "Did you do this?" To which Picasso replied, "No, you did!" Even so, Picasso was treated as a celebrity by the Occupation forces. This was another calculated display of propaganda, to advance the false narrative of benevolent, gentle occupiers by allowing even Picasso to continue producing his art.

Many booksellers as part of underground resistance took to hiding banned books, including Sylvia Beach at Shakespeare & Co. who was somewhat shielded from the initial wave of assault by her American nationality. Things changed for her bookstore in 1942 after the U.S. entered the war. Beach concealed most of her stock in an empty apartment above her shop, boarding up the entranceway and painting over the walls of dismantled shelves. When the Germans came to confiscate her stock of books, for their infamous bonfires, they found nothing. Even so, she was arrested in September 1942 as an enemy alien. She spent six months internment in Vittel, along with hundreds of other American women, and then returned to Paris. For the rest of the occupation, she kept her head down hoping to pass unnoticed. The glory days of Shakespeare & Co. were over.

What did all this mean for Yasushi and Louise? They were not famous enough, like Picasso, to be on the radar of the Germans. Technically, as a Japanese national, Yasushi would not be persecuted because of the military alliance between Germany, Italy and Japan. Louise was no longer an American citizen, and one has to wonder if she leveraged her mother's maiden name Gephard to avoid drawing attention. Like so many Paris citizens, they had no choice but to hunker down, muffle their opinions, and quietly try to survive.

Yasushi's Death Under Nazi Occupation

THAT FIRST WINTER OF 1940 was horribly cold, by all accounts. The Nazis were anything but the beneficial occupiers they had claimed to be. They strictly rationed all basic necessities which took a toll on the city's population. One wonders if they had enough coal to stoke the Godin stove that Ezra Pound had left behind in their semi-furnished apartment. Like many of their neighbors, the Tanakas likely spent much of their time at the cafe Coupole huddled around a public heater.

Tuberculosis was epidemic, and Yasushi fell victim to it. Without adequate nutrition or antibiotics to fight the disease, he spent the last months of his life wasting away, consumed from within by the ancient disease that devoured his lungs.

He lingered until the following spring and died at a nearby hospital, the historic *Hôpital Necker - Enfants malades* at 151 rue de Sevres, on April 24, 1941 at 10:40 PM. He was just one month short of his 56th birthday. The official death record that gives his date and place of death lists his occupation as artist-painter, misspells his parents' names as "Samuro Tanaka and Vigo," and lists his wife Louise Cann.

World War II

ON DECEMBER 7, 1941, the Japanese executed their surprise attack on the Navy shipyards of Pearl Harbor, Hawaii. On the following day, the United States declared war against the Empire of Japan. Yasushi passed away just seven months before the Japanese attack on Pearl Harbor. He never lived long enough to see his homeland and his wife's homeland declare war on each other. His untimely death spared him and Louise from deciding whether or not to flee Nazi-occupied Paris and, if they fled, where to go.

If they had returned to Seattle or San Francisco, or any city on the west coast of the U.S., then Yasushi would have been forcibly interred in a concentration camp. President Franklin D. Roosevelt issued Executive Order 9066 on February 19, 1942. This order authorized the Secretary of War to prescribe certain areas within the U.S. as military zones, placed under martial law, and authorized the mass incarceration of Japanese Americans. Primarily the targeted areas were on the Pacific Coast of the U.S. that had the majority of Japanese immigrants. Armed soldiers dragged over 100,000 people from their homes and confiscated their property. Whole families—including small children, many of whom were citizens born in the U.S.—were forcibly transported to concentration camps in remote desert areas.

Yasushi would have suffered the fate of many other Japanese-American artists uprooted from their homes and sent to desolate locations. Living under harsh conditions, under armed guard behind fences of barbed wire, and with little access to art supplies, the majority of West Coast artists had their health and creative spirit fundamentally obliterated. Only in rare cases did a handful of artists, like Henry Sugimoto, find the will to continue painting and sketching while incarcerated.

Louise would have faced a difficult choice as an ex-patriate American woman married to a Japanese man. She could either stay loyal to her husband or she could abandon him, divorce him, and apply to regain her U.S. citizenship. Another woman in similar circumstances, Estelle Peck Ishigo, chose to accompany her husband into the internment camp. She later wrote about her experiences in "Lone Heart Mountain" and was the subject of an Academy Award winning documentary (1990), *Days of Waiting: The Life & Art of Estelle Ishigo.*

If they had returned to the United States on the east coast, or any other region, the Tanakas would not be subject to Executive Order 9066. They may not have been incarcerated in a concentration camp, but their lives would be disrupted nonetheless. The relatively small number of Japanese living elsewhere in the U.S. experienced harassment by authorities and were generally shunned by their neighbors.

One example is the artist Yasuo Kuniyoshi, a contemporary of Yasushi who followed a similar life path. He also came to the U.S. alone at the age of seventeen, landing in Seattle without a clear purpose. He worked at menial jobs before relocating to Los Angeles, California where he attended school and discovered art classes. He studied at the California School of Art and Design for three years, then moved to New York to pursue his art career. He also fell in love with an American woman and married Katherine Schmidt in 1919 but the marriage ended with divorce in 1932.

Kuniyoshi continued to develop a distinctive painting style and became one of the preeminent Japanese artists of the 1920s and 1930s. Kuniyoshi also chaired the Arts Council of Japanese Americans for Democracy in partnership with Isamu Noguchi (the estranged American-born son of poet Yone Noguchi) who was a talented sculptor in his own right. Kuniyoshi and other Japanese-Americans in the New York area became outspoken critics of their home country's military aggression in China.

However, when the attack on Pearl Harbor occurred, he was declared an enemy alien. His bank account was impounded. His camera equipment and all his photographs were confiscated. Prevented from ever applying for U.S.

citizenship because of the restrictive immigration laws of the time, Kuniyoshi nevertheless considered himself an American in spirit. He whole-heartedly supported the Allied war effort and volunteered to broadcast "Voice of America" radio speeches to Japan praising American democracy.

If they had returned to Japan, Yasushi and Louise would have struggled to adapt to a whole new world. Not only did Louise have minimal knowledge of the difficult language and insular culture, but Yasushi had been away for more than thirty years. His country had rapidly transformed in his absence to be unrecognizable from the home he had left behind. His brothers were strangers.

Many other Japanese artists, who returned in the late 1930s from travels abroad, joined the cause of rising nationalistic patriotism. They did not fight on the front lines but rather their specialized talents were exploited into creating war propaganda, known as war art. One has to wonder if Yasushi would have cooperated with the pressure to paint such things for the propaganda efforts, given his American sensibilities and his rebellious individuality.

One example is Toshi Shimizu, who came to the U.S. two years after Yasushi had arrived. He also studied art in Seattle with Fokko Tadama for about ten years. Shimizu moved to New York City in 1917 where he studied at the Art Students League and worked as a painter. He faced similar incidents of discrimination in the U.S. that Yasushi had experienced, for example, winning a prize at the Art Institute of Chicago only to have the prize later revoked because he was not (and could never be) a U.S. citizen. A familiar, oft-repeated story by now, that East Asians were prohibited by federal law to naturalize as citizens, and their lack of U.S. citizenship became an excuse to exclude them from American art competitions. An article in *American Art News*, “Chicago Overrules Jury and Bars Jap” recounts the 1921 episode. Shimizu went on to Paris in 1924, again following in Yasushi's footsteps. His style gradually morphed from gritty urban realist subjects to the more abstract. Here is where his life's path diverges. He only stayed three years in Paris before returning home to Japan in 1927. He continued painting and stayed even as Japan became more militaristic. When the war machine got into full gear, he joined the leagues of his contemporaries in painting pro-militaristic, war propaganda scenes in the European style.

As another example, the famous Monsieur Fujita returned to Japan from his self-imposed exile in South America as the war drums began to beat. In his homeland, he became more notorious than he had been in Paris. He was by far the most prolific at creating war art—scenes of brave Japanese soldiers engaged in battle or valorous civilians honorably suffering mass tragedies. Fujita's propaganda art was reproduced on inspirational posters and flyers and circulated widely in the territories conquered by Japan. His post-war critics accused him of romanticizing the horror and stoking the fires of nationalistic patriotism. After Japan's defeat, most war artists disavowed themselves of their nationalistic patriotism, destroyed their own work or put it behind. Fujita remained unapologetic. He returned to France to live out the rest of his days in relative obscurity. His defiant pride led to Fujita being shunned for a generation. Only in recent years, he is being rediscovered—or perhaps forgiven—and his name is once more coming into the public view.

Nazi-Occupied Paris

LOUISE CONTINUED LIVING in Paris, in Ezra Pound's former apartment, throughout the bleak years of World War II. She focused on her own survival and preserving Yasushi's hundreds of paintings and sketchbooks as best she could. Her near-familial bond with the concierge of her apartment building was critical to her survival throughout the duration of the Nazi occupation. The keen eyes of the wise, matronly woman in the ground floor window guarded the residents as if they were her own. Stories of the Nazi occupation, as told in the book *When Paris Went Dark*, have numerous anecdotes of concierges—both good and bad. Some shuttled Jewish clients among empty apartments while others betrayed Jews to the Nazis and looted their belongings.

What little I know of Louise during the Nazi occupation, she performed a courageous act in giving shelter to a fellow named Raymond de Botton, a painter of Jewish ancestry. Born in Alexandria, Egypt, he went to France before the war and found himself stuck there for the duration. He was remarkably lucky to survive the occupation without being discovered. The Nazis had conducted surveillance for several years beforehand and made detailed lists of residents and business owners of Jewish heritage. During the occupation, they went door-to-door with surgical precision and seized Jews in their homes and businesses. Jewish people were rounded up in ever-increasing groups as the unopposed Nazis grew bolder. In broad daylight, they penned up thousands of people in a sports stadium before packing them into freight trains bound for extermination camps. Resistance fighters were too few to be effective; many were caught and publicly executed. The majority of Parisians kept quiet, kept their doors locked and their window shades drawn.

The circumstances are unknown of exactly when or how Raymond de Botton came to live in the Tanakas' apartment. It could be that he was another one of a long line of Yasushi's art students. The Tanakas never had children of their own, and it could be that Louise may have viewed Raymond as a kind of son she never had. Considering her strong-willed independent nature, of course she would have hidden him from certain death. Perhaps she quietly assisted Raymond with his underground resistance efforts, applying his art skills to creating forged documents to smuggle refugees out of the country.

Louise held on through the dark days of Nazi occupation for three whole years after losing Yasushi. In June 1944 the Allied forces stormed the beach of Normandy, France. The hopes of Parisians rose with the news. Then came the joyous day in August 1944 when American tanks rolled into Paris and Nazis surrendered control of the city. Yet it would be another long winter, the last one, until Hitler's defeat. Nazi Germany surrendered to the allies in May 1945.

The American forces concentrated the next six months in the Pacific to crush the last of Japan's fighting spirit but a swift Allied victory proved elusive. In the summer of 1945, the battles at Iwo Jima and Okinawa suffered high casualties as the Japanese continued to fight to the last one standing. The U.S. President Franklin Delano Roosevelt died of a stroke in April, and his Vice-President Harry S. Truman assumed the office. Faced with the option of conventional warfare or use of the newly developed thermo-nuclear "atom" bomb, Truman ordered the obliteration of the southern port cities Hiroshima and Nagasaki in the first week of August 1945. Truman is quoted, “The only language they seem to understand is the one we have been using to bombard them. When you have to deal with a beast you have to treat him as a beast.”

Even after the atomic bombs caused unspeakable destruction, many of the Japanese military wished to continue the fight. They were determined to make a futile stand down to the last man, woman, and child. Everyone in the civilian population had been preparing, with dread, for such a possibility. Farmer wives in the countryside trained with long sticks to use as spears for when the Yankees might invade.

Emperor Hirohito favored surrender over annihilation, and from a bunker underneath the Imperial household he pre-recorded his speech to the nation on a phonograph. Some attempted to prevent the recording. Shots were fired. Men died. The record disk was smuggled out of the palace and carried secretly to the studio of NHK Radio, where it was broadcast to the nation the following day, at noon on August 15, 1945.

The emperor's thin, tremulous voice was his first public radio broadcast. He addressed his citizens, literally, as the voice of a living god. In what is called the Jewel Voice Broadcast, the emperor gave a heartfelt plea, and command, for everyone to lay down arms in surrender. Yet his ultra-courtly, esoteric vocabulary was impossible for the majority of the population to understand, and confusion lingered for several minutes. Some wondered if the emperor intended for them to fight to the death—to every last man, woman, and child. Only when the radio announcer followed with a prepared, common-language translation of the emperor's proclamation did the meaning become clear.

The emperor described the horror of the atomic bomb and stated, "Should we continue to fight, not only would it result in an ultimate collapse and obliteration of the Japanese nation, but also it would lead to the total extinction of human civilization." He declared that Japan would accept the demands of the allied forces and surrender. "It is according to the dictates of time and fate that We have resolved to pave the way for a grand peace for all the generations to come by enduring the unendurable and suffering what is unsufferable.... Let the entire nation continue as one family from generation to generation, ever firm in its faith in the imperishability of its sacred land, and mindful of its heavy burden of responsibility, and of the long road before it... Unite your total strength, to be devoted to construction for the future. Cultivate the ways of rectitude, foster nobility of spirit, and work with resolution – so that you may enhance the innate glory of the imperial state and keep pace with the progress of the world." Millions of Japanese citizens wailed and wept in the streets. Yet the emperor had spoken and the people obeyed. At last, the war was over.

After the war, Louise remained in the same apartment studio at 70 bis, as curator and protector of her late husband's body of work. Hundreds of colorful canvases filled every available nook of the small space. Larger canvases stood stacked against the walls. Smaller pieces hung on every available wall space up to the rafters. Loose-leaf sketchbooks piled on shelves or in steamer trucks.

First order of business: Louise applied at the U.S. Embassy in Paris to regain her American citizenship that had been stripped away by the restrictive laws of thirty years before. Yet she chose to remain in France and never again returned to the land of her birth.

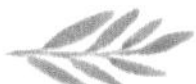

Louise Cann's Final Years

NOW A WOMAN IN HER 70s, she forged ahead with her literary pursuits. She devoted her energy to writing a fictionalized memoir of Paris during the Nazi Occupation, jumping on the bandwagon of so many others who published their eyewitness accounts of those dark days. The popular author Colette, who produced the Claudine novels and "Gigi," wrote her impressions in De ma Fenêtre (Paris From My Window). Unfortunately, Louise's manuscript, "The Agate Lamp," made the submission rounds but never managed to find a publishing house to pick it up.

It appears she continued living her life much in the same way she had always lived—an intelligent, highly literate woman at ease discussing philosophical topics over a glass of wine. She gave lively interviews to Richard Ellman, the biographer of James Joyce who had sought her out, and clearly recalled the brighter days of twenty years before, socializing at cafes and dancing to jazzy piano music.

Louise also contributed to the public-relations campaign spear-headed by Ernest Hemingway on behalf of Ezra Pound, the former occupant of her apartment. During the war, Pound had whole-heartedly embraced the fascist ideologies of Mussolini and Hitler while living in Italy. He made anti-American and anti-Semitic radio broadcasts which led to his arrest as a traitor and imprisonment for over a decade.

Louise wrote her commemoration piece in 1955, published in the *Pound Newsletter*, as a light-hearted, nostalgic piece. She mentioned none of his controversial political leanings, instead focusing on the man—the person she had known. Her public support for Ezra Pound has puzzled me. I wonder how she could compartmentalize Pound's actions during the war and his support for the facist regimes that were instrumental in her own husband's suffering death. Her article mentions none of it, so I am left to speculate that she took a similar viewpoint as Hemingway himself. Once he wrote to a colleague, Archibald MacLeish, in defense of Pound the man. "He deserves punishment and disgrace but what he really deserves most is ridicule. ...It is impossible to believe that anyone in his right mind could utter the vile, absolutely idiotic drivel he has broadcast."

One elemental truth had not changed from the day that she and Yasushi stepped foot in France: an apartment studio space in the Montparnasse district, on the Left Bank of Paris, would always be prime real estate in high demand. She received some financial assistance from the American Aid Society of Paris. To make ends meet, she rented extra space in the apartment to art students.

I learned about Louise's final years from my correspondence with one of her former tenants, Robert Short. He would later become a lecturer, historian, and author of a number of books on aspects of Surrealism. Back in 1955, Mr. Short was a youthful student on summer holiday a few months before starting his undergraduate years at Cambridge University. He planned to bicycle around France, staying in youth hostels along the way. A friend of the family urged him to look up "Mrs. Tanaka" in Paris at the end of the bicycle ride along the Loire Valley.

Mr. Short described to me bicycling over the cobbles from the Gare d'Austerlitz to the iron gate of 70 bis rue Notre Dame des Champs. The concierge led him up a long passage and across the courtyard to the door of the studio on the ground floor immediately beyond the yard with its door to an outside loo and almost life-size statue of a female nude partly covered with lichen and moss. "...I leave you to imagine my excitement when Mrs. Tanaka opened the door and invited me into the studio that first time. It was like everything I had read about bohemian Paris was right there before me. There was Tanaka art on all sides, right up to the high ceiling of the cube-shaped living room, hanging for the flight of narrow stairs that led to the single, exiguous bedroom over the hallway. A good part of the living space was taken up by an island on the side near the tiny back kitchen - an island of canvases stacked up metres thick and surrounded on all four sides by yet more Tanaka canvases. In front, stood a low table painted orange, supposedly constructed by the previous tenant, Ezra Pound, and covered with art periodicals and catalogues. There was a small (wicker-work) tea table and several wicker chairs with coloured cushions, one of which was always hers. Close by was the stove with its crooked chimney curling up to the ceiling. Beyond that was the alcove - a bit like a built-in conservatory - above which vertical windows went up to the ceiling level, giving a huge area of northern light. There was no bathroom or lavatory. The latter was across the courtyard. Like most in those days, it had no seat. It was shared with a fellow tenant, the sculptor, Ossip Zadkine.

"Mrs. Tanaka was instantly welcoming. She invited me to stay the night sleeping on the little balcony that abutted her bedroom. She sent me out to the corner store on the rue Vavin to buy a bottle of Saint Emilion, her favourite Bordeaux. She was very fond of wine and an inveterate smoker - I may be wrong on this but I seem to remember that she liked to roll her own. Things continued as they began that day. Mrs. Tanaka grasped at once that I was passionate about all things French. It was one of my favourite school subjects. I had several French novels in translation including Gide's 'The Coiners' which is largely set in Paris. I had won Ogrizek's illustrated guide to the provinces of France as a school prize. I'd seen a couple of René Clair's comedies at Sevenoaks School Film Club. And my first art love was the Impressionists. Things French for me then stood for freedom, in direct antithesis to the mores of an old-fashioned English boarding school! Knowing Mrs. Tanaka confirmed me in all of this.

"Mrs. Tanaka in the mid-fifties was still a sprightly, elderly lady. Physically, she was pretty thin and beaky, with sharp, intelligent eyes. Latterly, she walked out with the aid of a stick. She was up for taking me to museums and galleries like the Petit Palais, the Orangerie and the Musée Carnavalet, and out for coffee at the Coupole, the Dome and the Select on the Boulevard Montparnasse. Occasionally, we went together to double bills at the little Studio Parnasse cinema in the rue Jules Chaplain round the corner. She had lots of advice as to what I should see, not least the Sainte-Chapelle, and obviously, the Louvre.

She loved an opportunity to talk about her past, the artists she and Tanaka had known, how they had come to Paris and the scandal her divorce had caused in Seattle. When, over the years I spent either teaching in Paris or researching for my doctorate on surrealist politics, I took friends over to the studio, she was always welcoming and genuinely interested in what everyone was up to. It was obvious that she could make a very good journalist."

Over the next decade, Mr. Short continued making frequent visits to Paris, across the Channel, and although he never lodged with Louise after that first meeting, there was never a trip when he did not stop by to see her. "...Mrs. Tanaka never had much money. But her needs were modest. She ate frugally. Apart from the cigs and the claret, what she most enjoyed was reading, having people visit the studio, and talking about art. It was French art that she liked to talk about most: Chardin, Watteau, Géricault, Delacroix, Courbet... She had huge respect for Cézanne, Bonnard and Matisse. Léger she seldom mentioned though he was a near neighbour along the same road. It was some coincidence that the gate to 70 bis was bang opposite the studio of another painter of nudes, the 19th century academic painter, Bouguereau! I remember her quite often talking about the importance of 'tone' in painting, finding examples in the work of Tanaka close to hand.

"In the year 1960-61, I taught as an 'assistant d'anglais' at the Ecole Colbert near the Gare de l'Est. I rented a room on the ground floor of the building bang next door to Mrs. Tanaka's, namely 72, rue NotreDamedesChamps. A year or so later, when I was researching my doctorate, I lived at 8bis, Rue Campagne-Première, just a bit further off in Montparnasse."

Louise gave him several oil paintings as gifts. "When I was living in Paris, Mrs. Tanaka was in the habit of giving me work by her late husband, especially works on paper from one of the several folios that were to hand. She also gave single works to some of my friends when they came with me to call on her. She was ever so generous always, both with her time and her things." Louise confided in Mr. Short that Yasushi's style of painting fell out of trend in the years following the Second World War. As his widow, she did not have the means to aggressively promote his works with the vigor required to sell the unsellable. The latter half of the 20th century favored Surrealism—think of Salvadore Dali's analog clock melting over a tree branch, or René Magritte's painting of a man in a suit with a green apple floating in front of his face—and the Abstract Expressionism of Jackson Pollock with the splashes of paint across a canvas. Even the famous Leonard Foujita, who returned to France in 1955, could not revive his former fame; he lived out his final decade in relative obscurity.

In her later years, Louise was admitted to a nursing home in the town of Mennecy—a small commune roughly 25 miles (about 40 km) southeast of Paris. As Robert Short learned from corresponding with the former president of the American Aid Society, Louise received the society's aid from May 18, 1942 to May 1, 1947 and again from December 17, 1965 to June 7, 1966. During the gap between those dates, she was supported by some friends and the American journalist Janet Flanner. The American Aid Society ended their financial support in June 1966, so presumably she passed away around that time.

Upon her death, all of the belongings in the 70 bis apartment were tossed out, including her manuscript "The Agate Lamp" and whatever remained of her other writings. The Paris branch of the Bank of Saitama took possession of all the canvases—about two hundred pieces. The Tanaka collection went into storage for about a decade after Louise's death.

Some paintings and sketches came into the private collection of David Martin, an art dealer in Seattle for several decades along with his business partner Dominic Zambito. The two men have operated the gallery Martin-Zambito Fine Art since the 1980s that showcases Northwest regional artists, especially those who have been forgotten and merit rediscovery. Mr. Martin is the author of several books and has an esteemed reputation as an authority on the subject of early 20th century artists in the region.

Robert Short received gifts from Louise of a number of drawings, pastels, and oil paintings on canvas. By the early 1990s, Mr. Short began to consider reducing his collection of artwork, including the Tanaka pieces. He sold about 15 pastels and charcoal works on paper to Reiko Kurita, proprietor of the Galleria Graphica Tokyo, a contemporary art gallery founded in 1970 in the fashionable Ginza district of Tokyo, Japan. Also in the 1990s, while active as a senior lecturer in history at the University of East Anglia, in Norwich, England, he offered an additional five paintings for sale.

As referenced earlier, a representative of Mr. Matsukata purchased the painting of a "Nude" from Yasushi in 1924. Matsukata once had a grand vision of creating a national museum in Tokyo to showcase European arts, but financial troubles forced him to dispose of his extensive collection. Some 400 artworks in storage at the Musée Rodin, in Paris, were sequestrated by the French government toward the end of World War II as "enemy property" and held for more than a decade. Matsukata died in 1950 without ever realizing his dream of establishing a fine arts museum in Japan. In 1959, as a sign of the renewed amity between the two countries, the French returned the contents of the Matsukata Collection to Japan. The National Museum of Western Art *(Kokuritsu Seiyō Bijutsukan)* is located in Ueno Park in Tokyo.

The Museum of Modern Art (MOMA) opened in 1982 in Yasushi's hometown amid the lush greenery of Kita-Urawa Park. Over a dozen Tanaka pieces, including "Seated Woman in a Black Dress" and a self-portrait sketched in pencil, are on permanent display. Mr. Shizuo Okubo, art historian and former curator at MOMA-Saitama, flew to London and Paris in the early 1980s for personal meetings with Robert Short to gather a wealth of backgrounder information. Okubo also corresponded with David Martin in Seattle, Washington. Okubo compiled the results of these interviews, and his own research, into a retrospective catalogue of Yasushi Tanaka's work published by the museum's press in 1988. There are a few brief pages of biographical information, the majority of the slim hardcover being glossy full-color pages of the paintings. The Japanese title translates to "1920-30s Rhapsody in Paris: painter Yasushi Tanaka and his contemporaries."

A second museum in Japan currently holds a significant collection of Tanaka's artworks. The Satoe Memorial Art Museum of the 21st Century (SAMA) is located in the town of Kazo, about one hour north of Saitama City by train. The modest building is surrounded by a traditional-style Japanese garden decorated with a flowing stream, a koi fish pond, and about 20 sculptures. SAMA has also held several exhibitions over the years, ranging from contemporary artists to deceased artists from the local region. Their online store sells packets of postcards and exhibit catalogs including several of Yasushi Tanaka's works.

Today, there may be a few scattered pieces in the hands of private collectors, but the majority of Yasushi's body of work is housed in a museum in his hometown Saitama, a suburb of Tokyo. His legacy stands apart, unique as a Japanese-American artist of Paris.

Acknowledgements

My very special thanks go to Robert Short, with the Norfolk Contemporary Art Society, who generously shared his personal recollections of Louise G. Cann (a.k.a. "Mrs. Tanaka") in the later years of her life.

I am grateful for the kind assistance of those who responded to my inquiries: Meg Partridge, Director, Imogen Cunningham Trust; Jane Glover, Coordinator, American Art Study Center at the Fine Arts Museums of San Francisco; Itaru Oura, curator at the Museum of Modern Art, Saitama, Japan; and Morgan Rhodes and Manuela de Botton Davidson.

ILLUSTRATIONS

by Yasushi Tanaka, 1913
Courtesy of Museum of History & Industry, Seattle (MOHAI)

- Fig. 12 Yasushi Tanaka and Louise Cann, circa 1919
From The Seattle Star, August 29, 1919
- Fig. 13 Portrait of the Arctic Explorer Stefansson
From the Seattle Sunday Times, October 12, 1919
- Fig. 14 Brochure of Yasushi Tanaka's Farewell Exhibition, January 1920
Courtesy of Lewis & Clark College Special Collections and Archives
- Fig. 15 Photograph portrait of Yasushi Tanaka, circa 1920
From Yasushi Tanaka letters to Frederic C. Torrey, 1913-1924.
Courtesy of Archives of American Art, Smithsonian Institution
- Fig. 16 Art Reviews and News clipping(s) of Yasushi Tanaka, in Paris, Including the Artist's Handwritten Margin Comments
From Yasushi Tanaka letters to Frederic C. Torrey, 1913-1924.
Courtesy of Archives of American Art, Smithsonian Institution
- Fig. 17 "Artist in Studio"
From ArtNet
- Fig. 18 Photograph Portrait of Writer-Journalist Janet Flanner, in Paris, 1924,
with the portrait in the background of Solita Solano painted by Yasushi Tanaka
Courtesy of the Library of Congress, the Janet FlannerSolita Solano papers
- Fig. 19 Photograph Portrait of Yasushi Tanaka, circa 1935-1940
Courtesy of Robert Short, personal collection
- Fig. 20 Raymond Botton with Louise Tanaka, at her Paris apartment, circa 1950
From blog Learning2Leap, "Buckley's trash, My treasure"
- Fig. 21 Robert Short with Louise Tanaka, at her Paris apartment, circa 1960
From blog Photo Utopia, "Yasushi Tanaka's studio 1960"

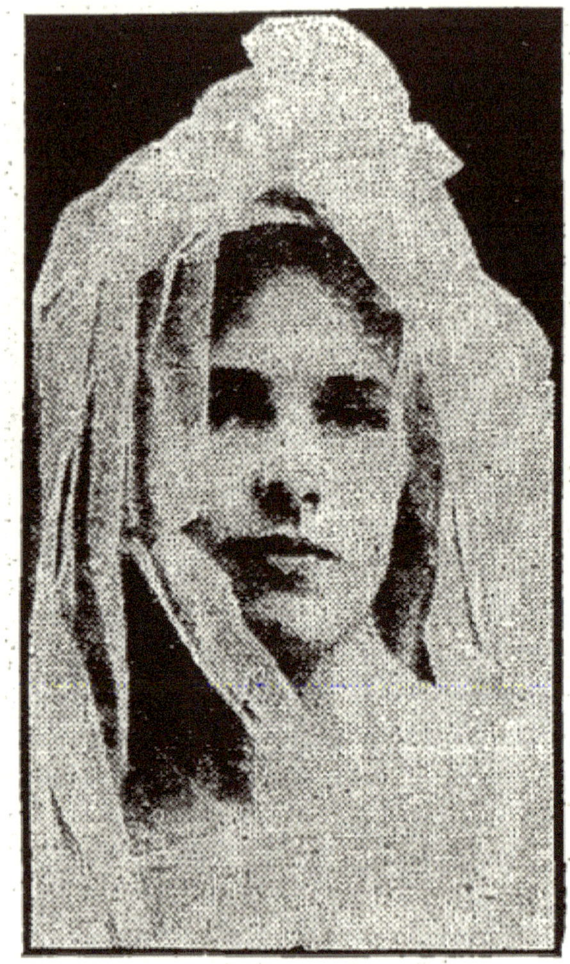

Fig. 1

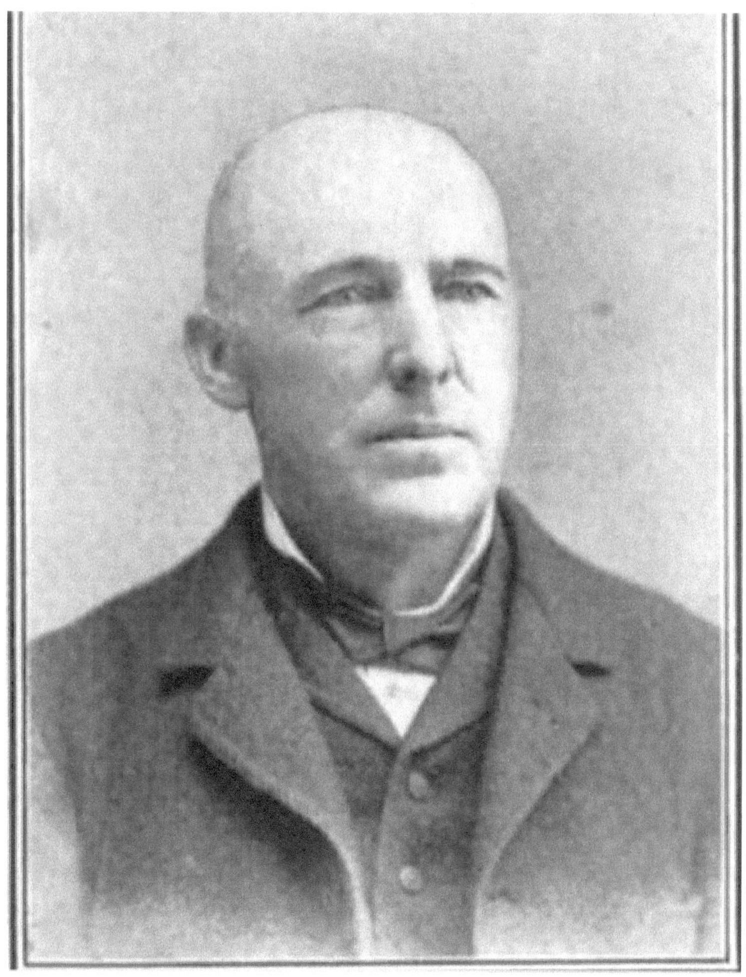

Fig. 2

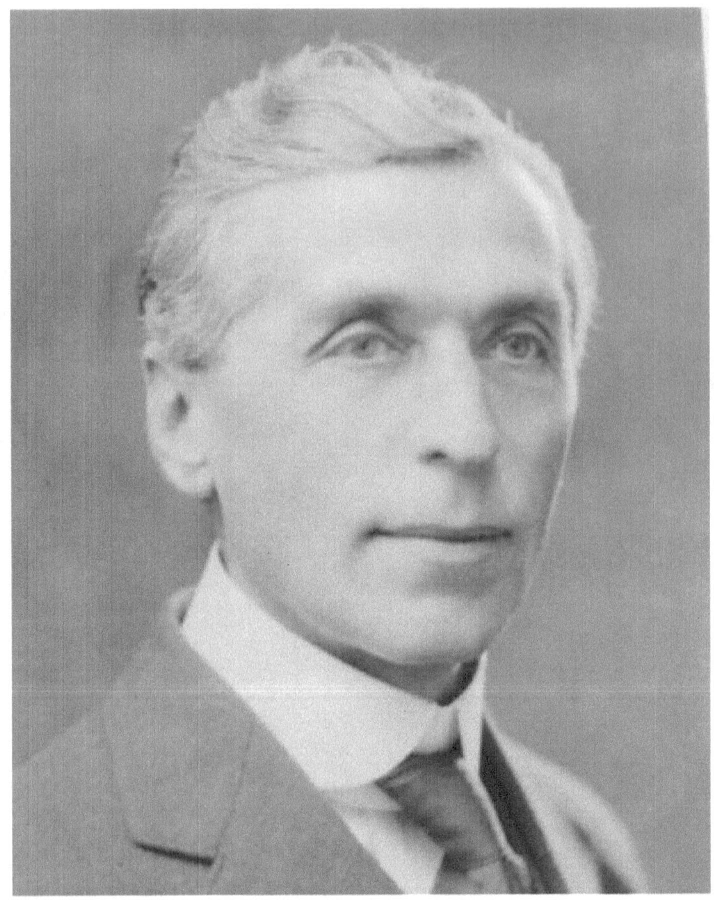

Fig. 3

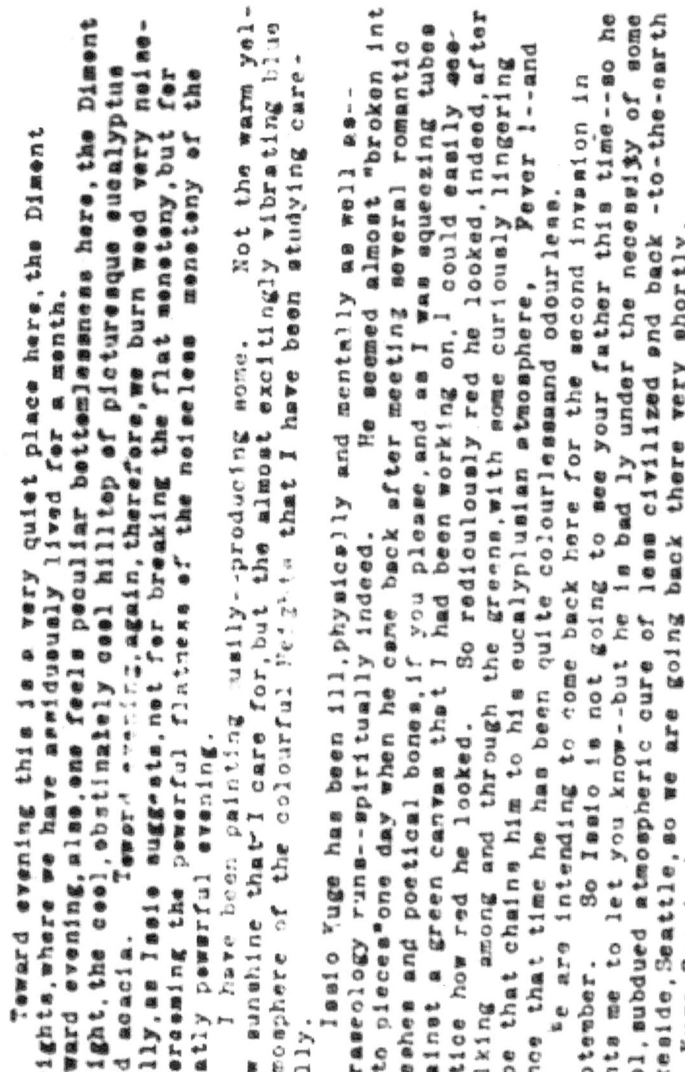

Toward evening this is a very quiet place here, the Diment Heights, where we have assiduously lived for a month.
Toward evening, also, one feels peculiar bottomlessness here, the Diment Height, the cool, obstinately cool hilltop of picturesque eucalyptus and acacia. Toward evening, again, therefore, we burn weed very noisefully, as Issio suggests, not for breaking the flat monotony, but for overcoming the powerful flatness of the noiseless monotony of the flatly powerful evening.

I have been painting busily--producing some. Not the warm yellow sunshine that I care for, but the almost excitingly vibrating blue atmosphere of the colourful Heights that I have been studying carefully.

Issio Kuge has been ill, physically and mentally as well as--phraseology runs--spiritually indeed. He seemed almost "broken int into pieces" one day when he came back after meeting several romantic fleshes and poetical bones, if you please, and as I was squeezing tubes against a green canvas that I had been working on, I could easily see notice how red he looked. So rediculously red he looked, indeed, after walking among and through the greens, with some curiously lingering hope that chains him to his eucalyplusian atmosphere, Fever !--and since that time he has been quite colourlessand odourless.

We are intending to come back here for the second invasion in September. So Issio is not going to see your father this time--so he wants me to let you know--but he is bad ly under the necessity of some cool, subdued atmospheric cure of less civilized and back -to-the-earth Lakeside, Seattle, so we are going back there very shortly.

Kuge San is heavily quiet, so I snatched his pen.

Very truly yours,

Fig. 4

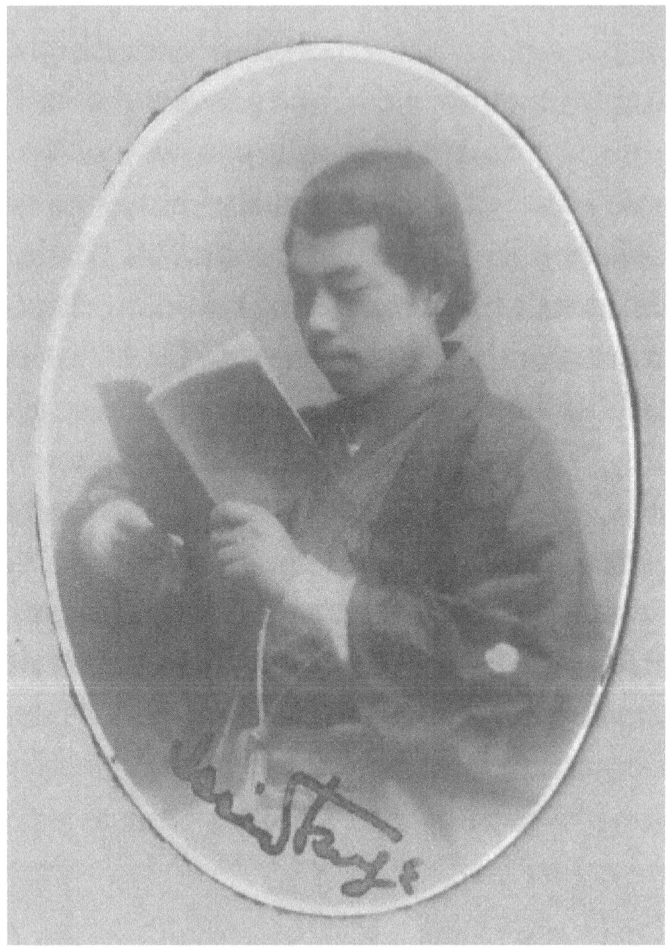

Fig. 5

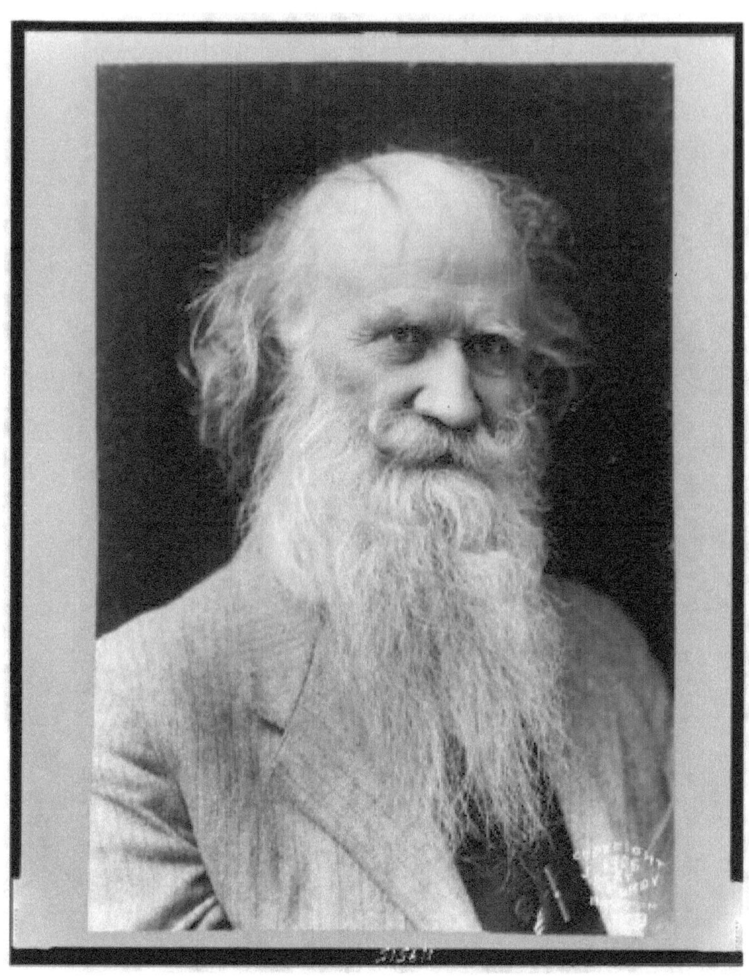

Fig. 6

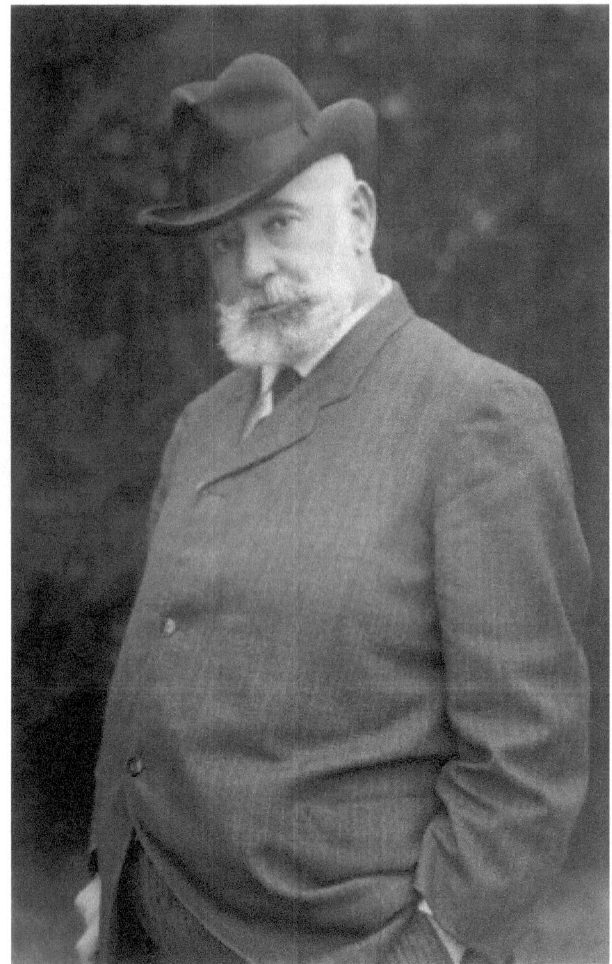

Fig. 7

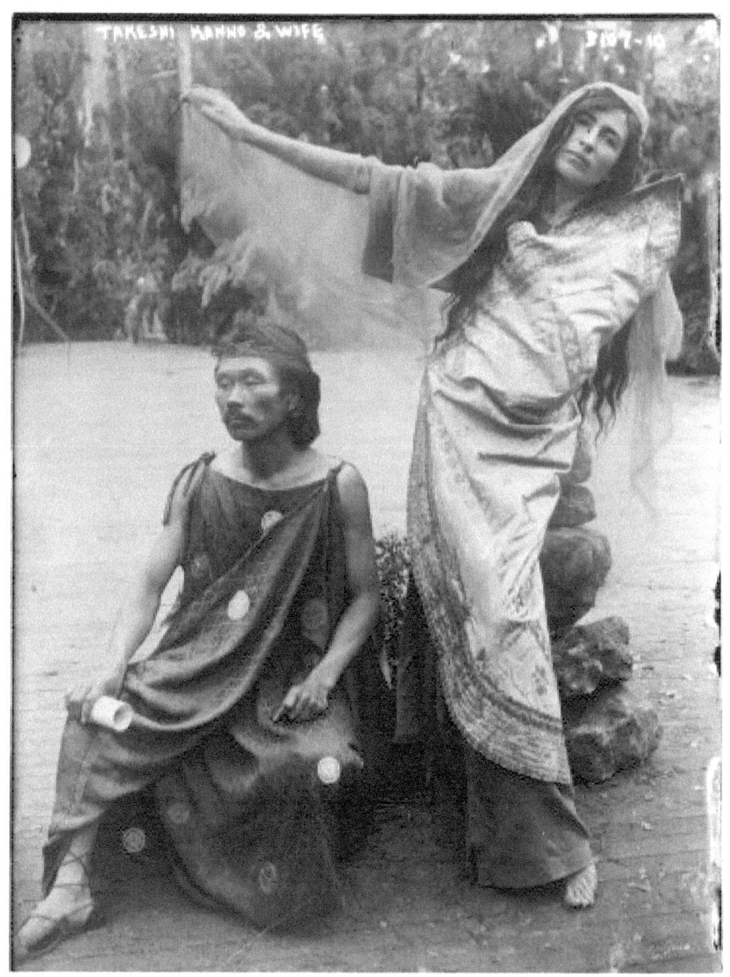

Fig. 8

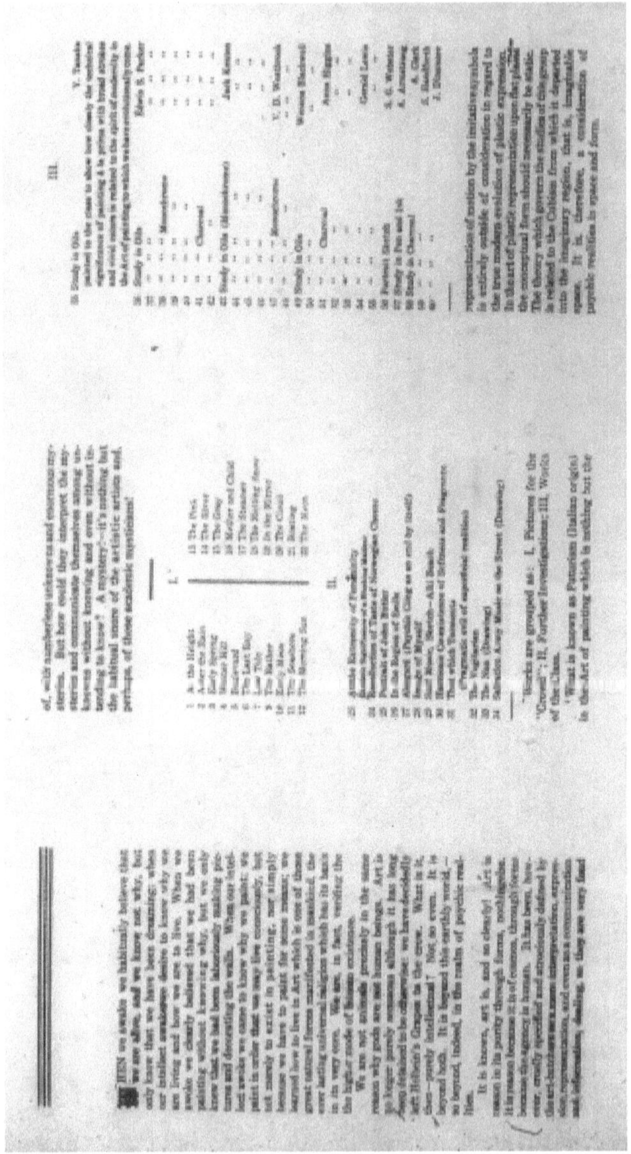

Fig. 9

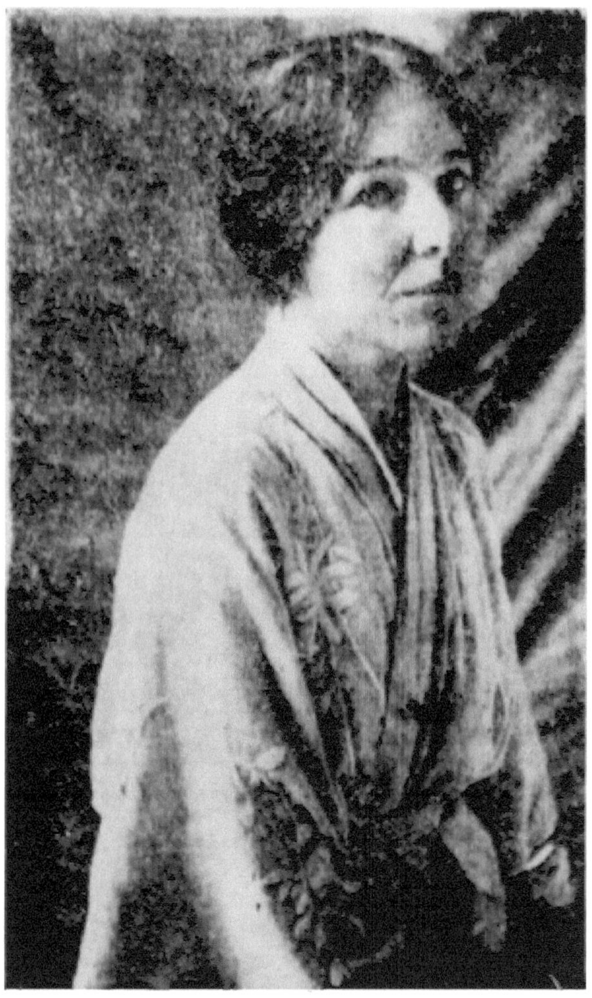

Fig. 10

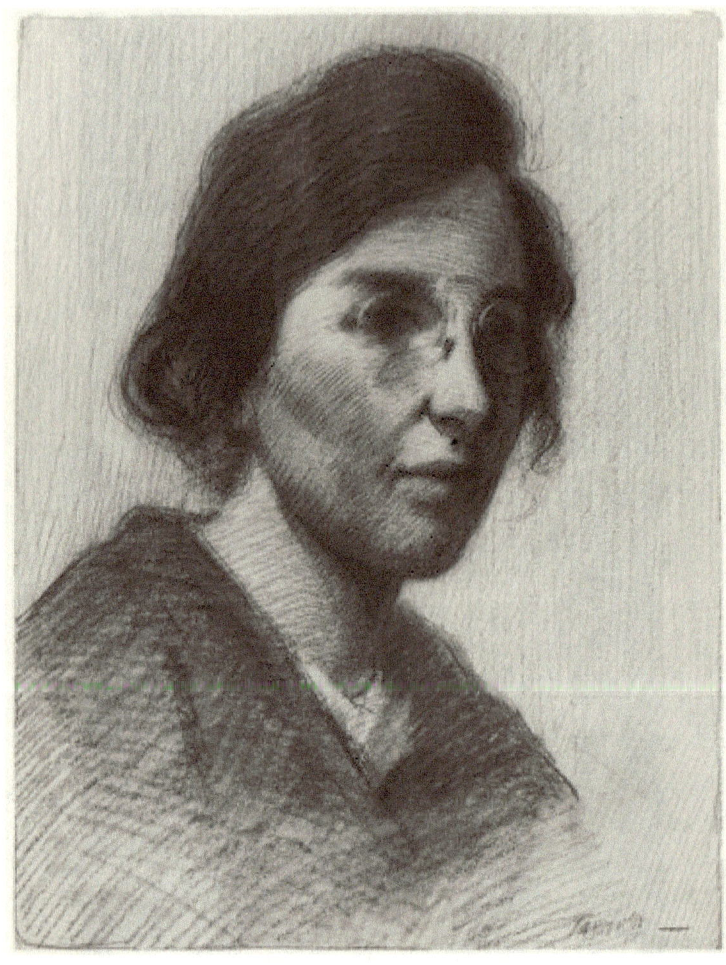

Fig. 11

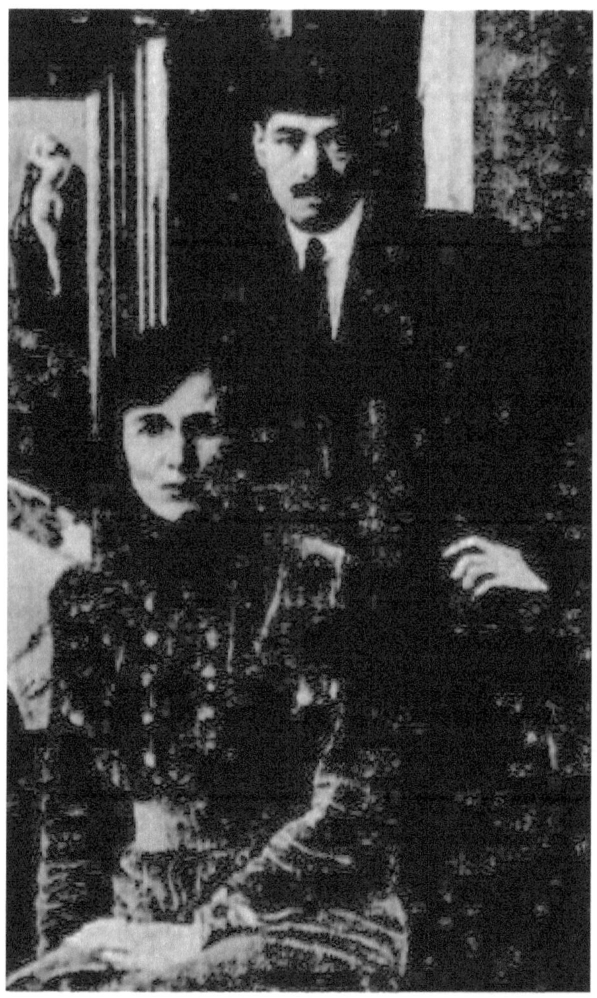

Fig. 12

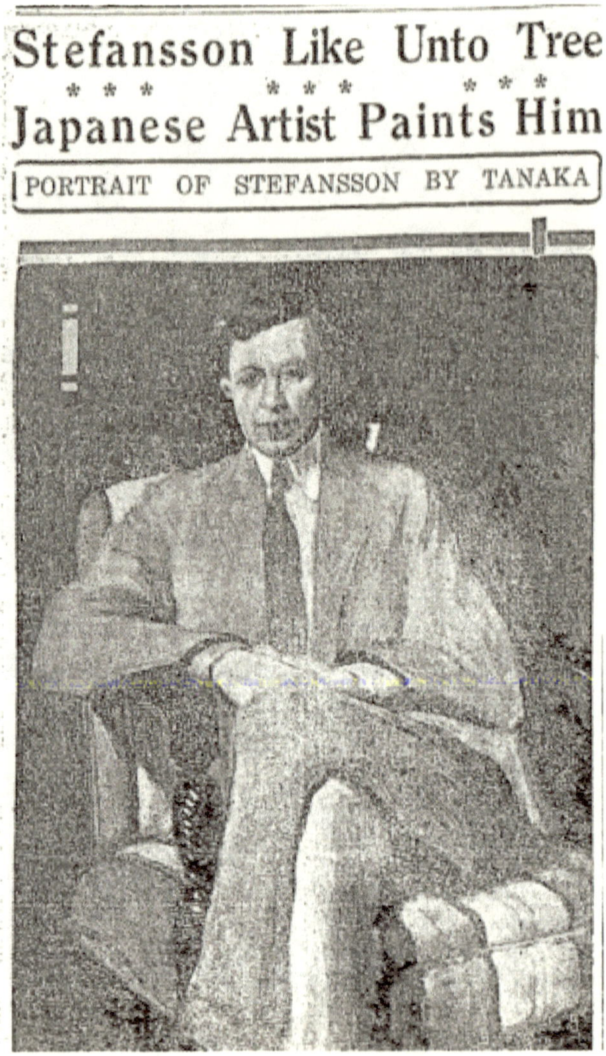

Stefansson Like Unto Tree

* * * * * * * * *

Japanese Artist Paints Him

PORTRAIT OF STEFANSSON BY TANAKA

Fig. 13

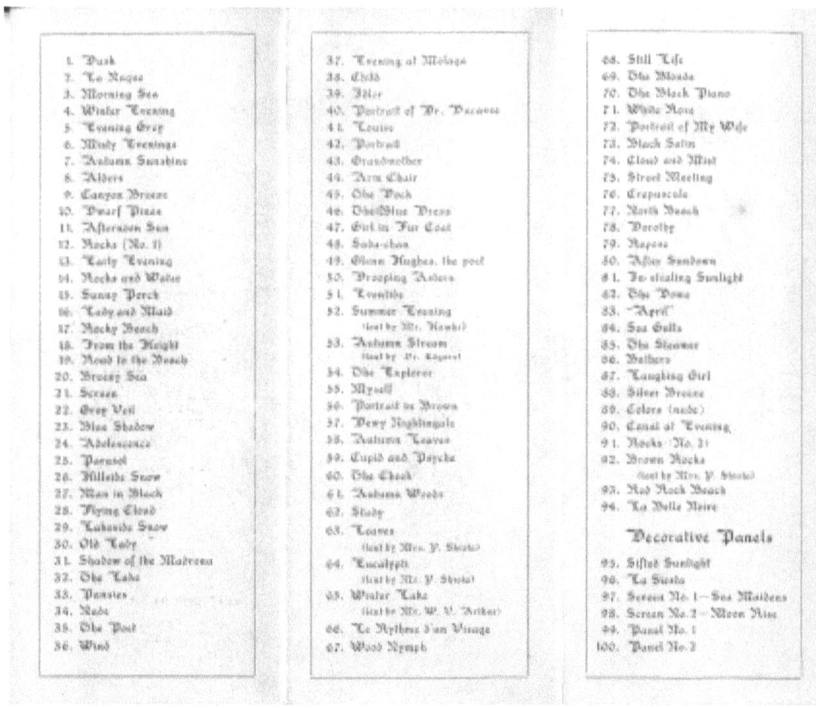

1. Dusk
2. La Vague
3. Morning Sea
4. Winter Evening
5. Evening Gray
6. Misty Evenings
7. Autumn Sunshine
8. Alders
9. Canyon Breeze
10. Dwarf Pines
11. Afternoon Sun
12. Rocks (No. 1)
13. Early Evening
14. Rocks and Water
15. Sunny Porch
16. Lady and Maid
17. Rocky Beach
18. From the Height
19. Road to the Beach
20. Breezy Sea
21. Screen
22. Grey Veil
23. Blue Shadow
24. Adolescence
25. Parasol
26. Hillside Snow
27. Man in Black
28. Flying Cloud
29. Lakeside Snow
30. Old Lady
31. Shadow of the Madrona
32. The Lake
33. Pansies
34. Nude
35. The Poet
36. Wind
37. Evening at Malaga
38. Child
39. Idler
40. Portrait of Dr. [illegible]
41. Louise
42. Portrait
43. Grandmother
44. Arm Chair
45. The Dock
46. The Blue Dress
47. Girl in Fur Coat
48. Sada-chan
49. Glenn Hughes, the poet
50. Drooping Asters
51. Eventide
52. Summer Evening
    (lent by Mr. Hawks)
53. Autumn Stream
    (lent by Dr. [illegible])
54. The Explorer
55. Myself
56. Portrait in Brown
57. Dewy Nightingale
58. Autumn Leaves
59. Cupid and Psyche
60. The Cloak
61. Autumn Woods
62. Study
63. Leaves
    (lent by Mrs. F. [illegible])
64. Eucalypti
    (lent by Mr. F. [illegible])
65. Winter Lake
    (lent by Mr. W. V. Arthur)
66. Le Rythme d'un Visage
67. Wood Nymph
68. Still Life
69. The Blonde
70. The Black Piano
71. White Rose
72. Portrait of My Wife
73. Black Satin
74. Cloud and Mist
75. Street Meeting
76. Crepuscule
77. North Beach
78. Dorothy
79. Repose
80. After Sundown
81. In-stealing Sunlight
82. The Dome
83. "April"
84. Sea Gulls
85. The Steamer
86. Bathers
87. Laughing Girl
88. Silver Breeze
89. Colors (nude)
90. Canal at Evening
91. Rocks (No. 2)
92. Brown Rocks
    (lent by Mrs. F. [illegible])
93. Red Rock Beach
94. La Belle Noire

Decorative Panels

95. Sifted Sunlight
96. La Siesta
97. Screen No. 1—Sea Maidens
98. Screen No. 2—Moon Rise
99. Panel No. 1
100. Panel No. 2

Fig. 14

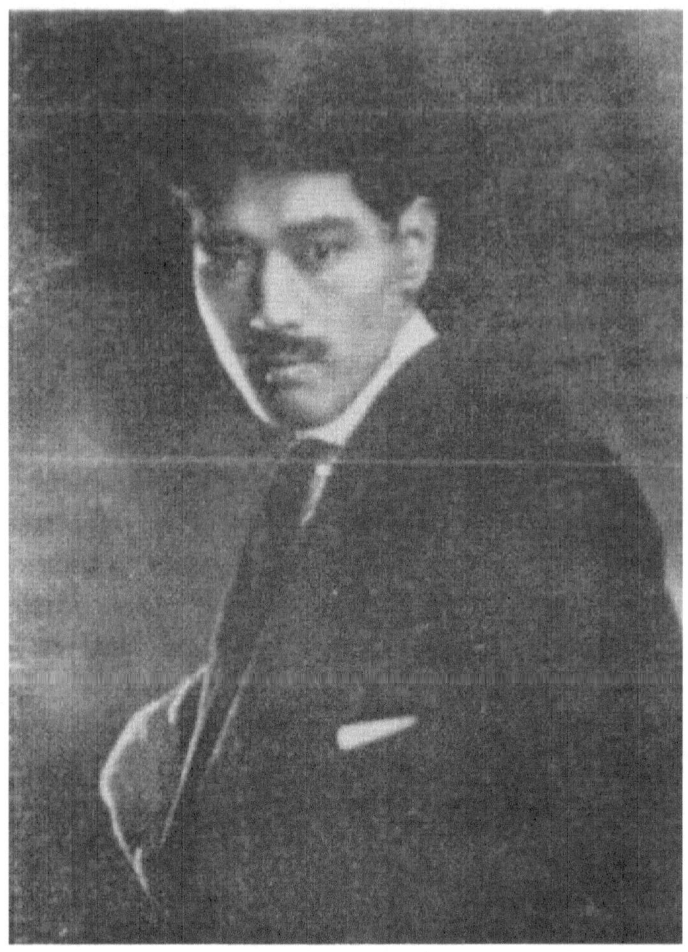

Fig. 15

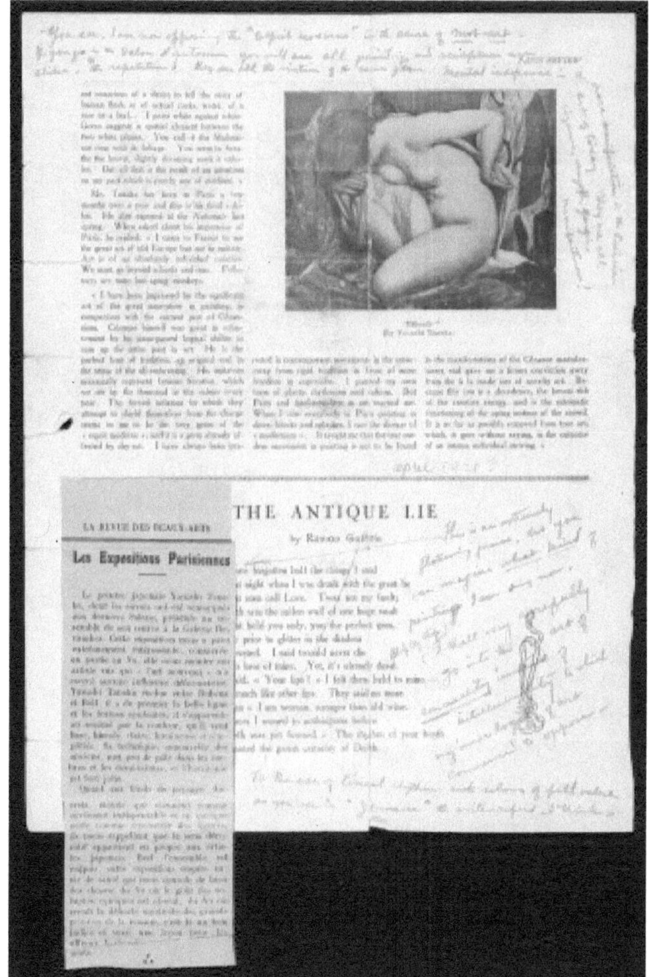

LA REVUE DES BEAUX-ARTS

Les Expositions Parisiennes

THE ANTIQUE LIE

Fig. 16

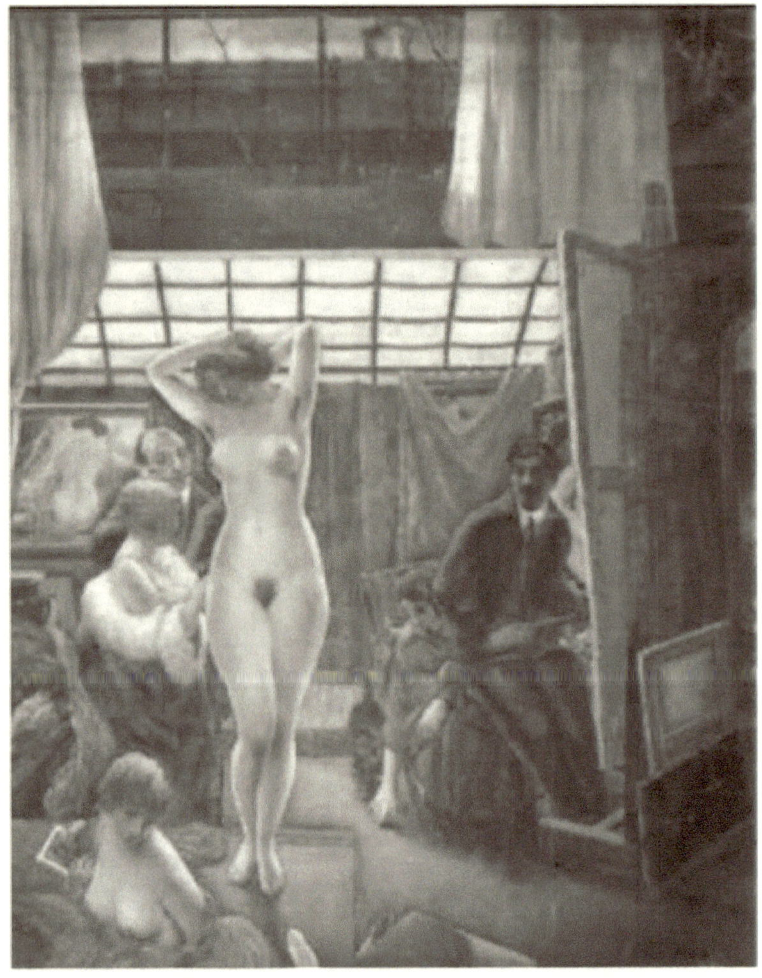

Fig. 17

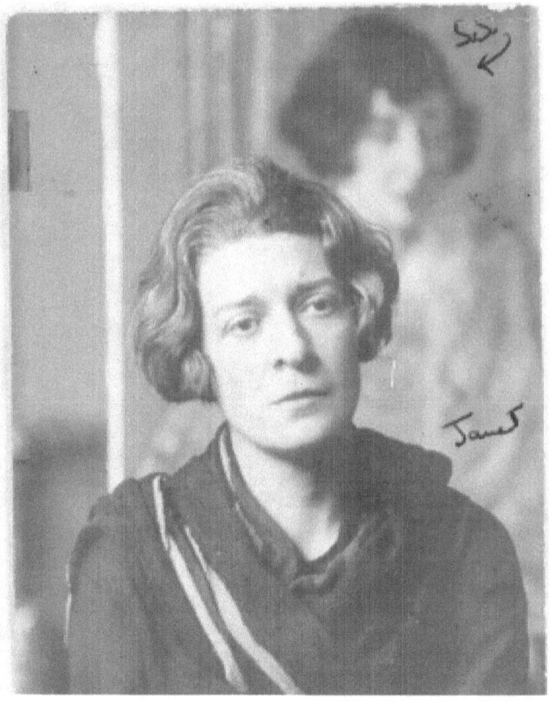

Fig. 18

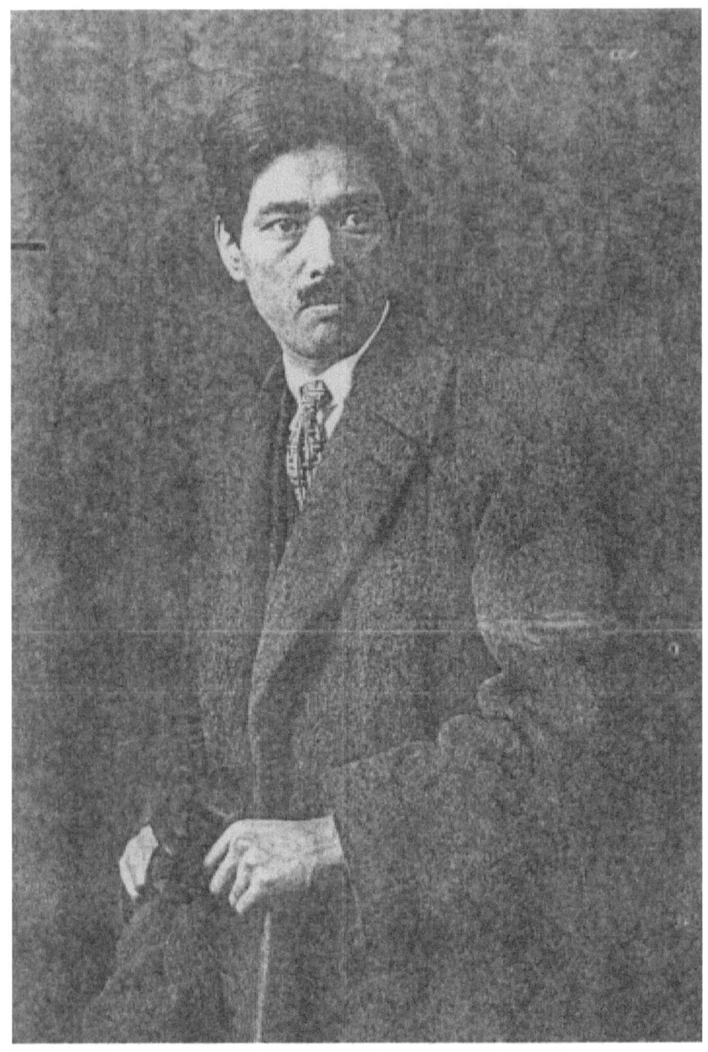

Fig. 19

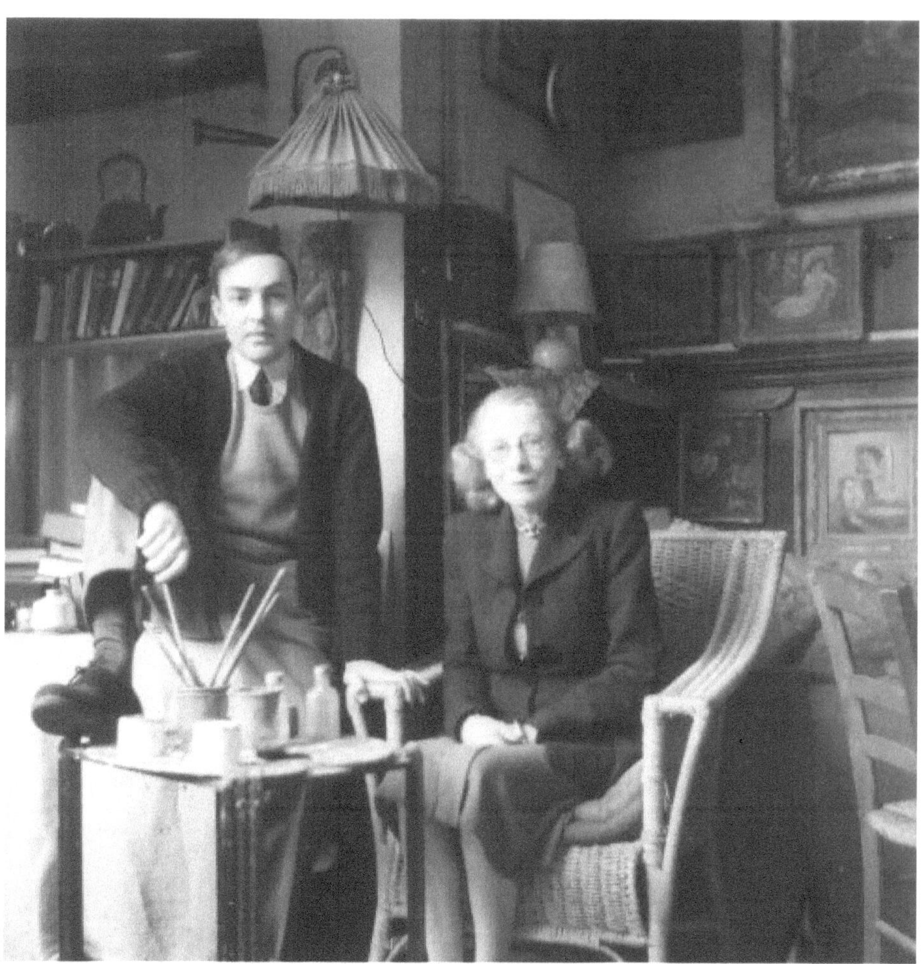

Fig. 20

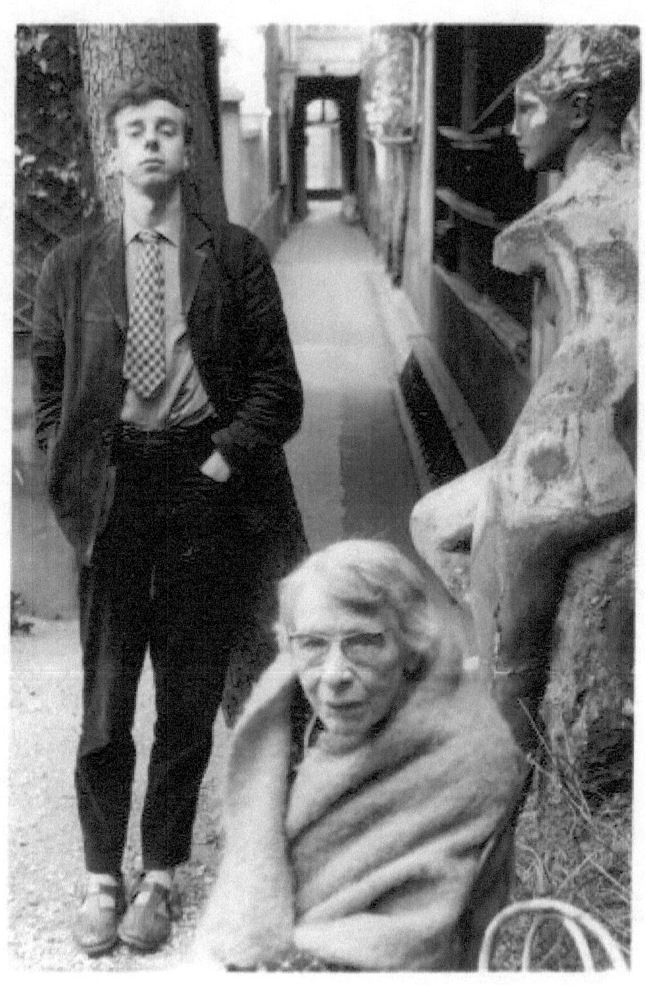

Fig. 21

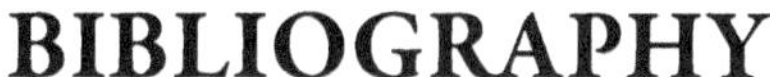

BIBLIOGRAPHY

Original and Rare Documents in Special Collections

My personal email correspondence with Robert Short (Dec. 2018 - Jan. 2019) including the gift of his essay dated 10/14/1994, his letters to curators of the Saitama museum in Japan, and his scrapbook items

My personal email correspondence with Meg Partridge, granddaughter of Imogen Cunningham and current trustee of the Imogen Cunningham Trust (Jan. 2019)

Civil, historical, and genealogical records too numerous to list in detail here. They are identified in the text, where cited. Digital records were accessed on Ancestry.com, FamilySearch.org, PERSI/Heritage Quest, the U.S. National Archives and Records Administration (NARA), the Oregon Historical Society (OHS), and Find-A-Grave.

Yasushi Tanaka's death record, 24 April 1941, Paris. Accessed directly on the France civil archives website. [https://www.service-public.fr]

Yasushi Tanaka letters to Frederic C. Torrey, 1913-1924, Archives of American Art, Smithsonian Institution, Microfilm reel 5474; frames 760-872 available at Archives of American Art offices. I viewed them at the DeYoung Museum in San Francisco, CA.

Louise Tanaka letters to Richard Ellman, The University of Tulsa. Richard Ellman Papers, Series 1, Research Files A - Z, Collection 1988-012.

Correspondence of Vilhjalmur Stefansson (1895-1962) Stefansson MSS-196, Box 9, Folder 21, Dartmouth College.

"With the Pounds in Paris," a Memoir by Louise Gebhard Cann. pp. 24 The Pound Newsletter, edited by J. Edwards, issue No. 8, October 1955 (at Stanford University, special collections, Felton Collection)

"Diary, Oct. 28-31, 1905." The personal journal of Charles Warren Stoddard, on a short stay at "The Hights" - residence of Joaquin Miller.

(Microfilm) Held at Duke University Libraries, Perkins Library, Durham, NC. OCLC No. 176868499.

"Letters of Issio Kuge." Charles Warren Stoddard Papers, call no. BANC MSS C-H 53, Box 1, Folder 11. University of California - Berkeley, Bancroft library.

"Farewell Exhibition of One Hundred Paintings by Yasushi Tanaka," original brochure with a catalog of paintings. Sleeth family collection. Series 1, Dana Sleeth Personal Ephemera, 1891-1936, Box 1, Folder 6, Item 6.24. Lewis & Clark College, Portland, OR.

"Martinez, Elsie, 1890-1984, interviewee." San Francisco Bay Area writers and artists: oral history transcript / Elsie Martinez; tape recorded interview conducted by Willa K. Baum and Franklin D. Walker in 1962-1963. Regional Oral History Office, The Bancroft Library, University of California, Berkeley, California, 1969: and related material, 1962-1969.

Newspapers, Periodicals

Articles in historical newspapers and periodicals, cited in text. Articles were accessed through the following websites: Library of Congress *Chronicling America*, Google Books, JSTOR.org, Hathi Trust Mobile Digital Library, Seattle Public Library, University of Washington, and online archives of the *New York Times* and *Seattle Times* newspapers.

Books in Print

Wolpert, Martin. Figurative Paintings, Paris and the Modern Spirit. Schiffer Pub. Ltd., February 1, 2006.

Riding, Alan. And the Show Went On: Cultural Life in Nazi-Occupied Paris. Vintage; Reprint edition (October 4, 2011)

Sueyoshi, Amy H. Queer Compulsions: Race, Nation, and Sexuality in the Affairs of Yone Noguchi. University of Hawaii Press, February 29, 2012

Lorenz, Richard. Imogen Cunningham: Ideas Without End, A Life and Photographs (paperback edition) Publisher: Chronicle Books (August 1, 1993)

Terasaki, Gwen. Bridge to the Sun. University of North Carolina Press, 1957.

Flanner, Janet. Paris Was Yesterday (1925-1938). New York : Viking Press, 1972

Asian American Art: A History, 1850-1970. Gordon H. Chang, Mark Dean Johnson, Paul J. Karlstrom. Stanford University Press, 2008

Inoue, Teiji. Tanaka Yasushi Kaleidoscope: the Mysterious Genius Artist and 1920s era Paris. Gallerie Hongo, Tokyo. May 1, 2000. (Japanese)

1920-30's Rhapsody in Paris : painter Yasushi Tanaka and his contemporaries. Edited and published by the Museum of Modern Art, Saitama. 1988. (Japanese/English)

Birnbaum, Phyllis. Glory in a Line: A Life of Foujita—the Artist Caught Between East and West. Farrar, Straus and Giroux; First edition (November 13, 2007)

Rothman, Richard. When Paris Went Dark: The City of Light Under German Occupation, 1940-1944 Back Bay Books; Reprint edition (March 17, 2015)

Newell, Gordon. SOS North Pacific; tales of shipwrecks off the Washington, British Columbia and Alaska coasts. Portland, OR, Binfords & Mort [1955]

Hemingway, Ernest. A Moveable Feast, The Restored Edition. Scribner, 2009.

Ellmann, Richard. James Joyce. Oxford University Press, 1959. New and Revised Edition 1982. pp. 491

A Volume of memoirs and genealogy of representative citizens of the city of Seattle and county of King, Washington: including biographies of many of those who have passed away. By Anonymous. Lewis Pub. Co., New York, 1903. pp. 237-240. Sourced from Heritage Quest

History of Seattle, From the Earliest Settlement to the Present Time, by Clarence B. Bagley, Vol. II, The S. J. Clarke Publishing Company, Chicago. 1916. pp. 853-857. Sourced from Heritage Quest

Websites

Learning2Leap (blog) Sunday, January 22, 2012, "Buckley's trash, My treasure." http://firstleaps.blogspot.com

Photo Utopia (blog) Monday, September 07, 2015, "Yasushi Tanaka's studio 1960" http://photo-utopia.blogspot.com/2015/09/yasushi-tanakas-studio-1960.html

"The Matsukata Collection." National Museum of Western Art, Tokyo. http://www.nmwa.go.jp/en/about/matsukata.html

The Museum of Modern Art, Saitama, Japan. http://www.pref.spec.ed.jp/momas

The Satoe Memorial Art Museum of 21st Century, in Saitama, Japan. http://www.satoe-museum.or.jp

U.S. National Park Service. The 1915 San Francisco Pan-Pacific International Expo. https://www.nps.gov/goga/learn/historyculture/ppie.htm

Journal Articles

"Art and Architecture Towards Political Crises: The 1937 Paris International Exposition in Context." https://culturedarm.com/1937-paris-international-exposition

"Confrontation" http://www.arthurchandler.com/paris-1937-exposition/

"The Sculpture of Frederick Shrady" by Paul Horgan. From "The Critic" vol. 25, the *Journal of Thomas More Association*, April - May 1967, pp. 60 - 65. http://shrady.net/articles/Paul%20Horgan%20Article.pdf

"The Loss of SS State of California, Gambier Bay, Alaska, August 1913," by Steve Lloyd. *The Sea Chest: Journal of the Puget Sound Maritime Historical Society*, Vol. 43, No. 1, September 2009, pp. 14

"Mobs Forcibly Expel Most of Seattle's Chinese Residents Beginning on February 7, 1886," by Phil Dougherty, Posted 11/17/2013, HistoryLink.org Essay 2745

"Yasushi Tanaka and Joyce's Encounters with Japan in Paris" by Kumiko Yamada, *Journal of Irish Studies*, Vol. 17, Japan and Ireland (2002), pp. 151-161 sourced from JSTOR Archive (http://www.jstor.org/pss/20533492)

American Art News, ranging from 1917 to 1922, vol. 16 (issues no. 11, 14, 16), vol. 18 (issues no. 12 and 18), vol. 19 (issues no. 29 and 30), vol. 20 (issues 6 and 12), and vol. 21 (issue no. 4) sourced from JSTOR

Overland Monthly, Vol. XLV, Jan - June 1905, pp. 526-628, "From the Mississippi to the Valley of the Sacramento: Memories of Fifty Years by Judge T. H. Cann of Seattle, Wash." sourced on Google Books

"Writers of the Day," (a brief profile of Louise Cann) *The Writer*, Volume 26, December 1914, No. 12, editor William Henry Hills pp. 181-182. sourced on Google Books

"The group of classes of Congruent Matrices with Application to the Group of Isomorphisms of Any Abelian Group," Arthur Ranum, 1906. Ph.D. Dissertation that includes a brief autobiography, sourced on Google Books

"Beaux Arts and Expositions, Yasushi Tanaka at Devambez.", by Louisgarde. pp. 15-16. 1921. *The Paris Review*. (digitized and available online at http://www.aaa.si.edu/collections/yasushi-tanaka-letters-to-frederic-c-torrey-10832)

"A Travers les Expositions: L'Exposition Yasushi Tanaka." pp. 81-83. *L'Art et les Artists*. Paris. Armand Dayot, founder/editor. Tome IV, No. 20 (Oct. 1921) to No. 24 (Feb. 1922) in French. https://gallica.bnf.fr

"State Supreme Court denies citizenship for UW School of Law graduate Takuji Yamashita on October 22, 1902," by David Wilma, posted 12/7/2000, HistoryLink.org Essay 2870

"When Saying 'I Do' Meant Giving Up Your U.S. Citizenship," by Meg Hacker, Spring 2014, Prologue Magazine, a quarterly publication of NARA—the U.S. National Archives and Records Administration, archives https://www.archives.gov/publications/prologue/2014/spring

The Original Writings of Louise Gebhard Cann (a.k.a. Mrs. Tanaka)

"Yasushi Tanaka," by L. Gebhard Cann. *The International Studio*, Volume 65, No. 259, pp. 89-96. September 1919. New York Offices of the International Studio. Editors: Charles Holme, Guy Eglington, Peyton Boswell, William Bernard McCormick, Henry James Whigham. Sourced on Google Books

"Eugene Lawrence Vail, 1857 - 1934" Exposition Retrospective, Galerie Jean Charpentier, Paris. 1937. (Worldcat.org OCLC number 4915827)

"The Present Literary Movement in France," by Louise Gebhard Cann. The Pacific Review. University of Washington Press, Seattle. Vol. I, June 1920 - March 1921. p. 493. Sourced on Google Books.

"Annette," (a short story) by Louise Cann Ranum, published in *National Magazine*, Volume 25, Issue 4, Editors Arthur Wellington Brayley, Joe Mitchell

Chapple, Contributor Arthur Wilson Tarbell, Bostonian publishing Company, 1907. Sourced on Google Books

Dreams. (collection of original poetry) Louise Cann Ranum, Poet Lore Company, 1910. Sourced on Google Books

"The Reader Critic: Let Them Fight It Out!" by Louise Gebhard Cann. Published in The Little Review: Literature Drama Music Art. Vol. 3, No. 9, pp. 20. New York, Margaret C. Anderson, 1917. Sourced through The Modernist Journals Project. http://www.modjourn.org/render.php?view=mjp_object&id=LittleReviewCollection

"Life is Always the Same," a drama in one act, by Louise Gebhard Cann, published in *The Drama, A Quarterly Review Devoted to the Drama*, No. 34, Dramatic Publishing Company, May 1919. Sourced on Google Books

"Monticelli" Monticelli's baffling legend : less is known of this immortal painter's real life that that of Francis Villon" by Louise G. Cann. New York: *The International Studio*, Vol. LXXVI, No. 306, p. 95. Nov. 1922.

"Jean Marchand—Neo-Classicist," by Louise Gebhard Cann. *The International Studio.* Vol. LXXV, No. 302, p. 321. July 1922.

Appendix

There are three items listed as references in the bibliography of the book 1920-30's Rhapsody in Paris (cited above) that I am unable to find in the original.

- Hayashi, Kiichiro, "Forgotten Painter, Yasushi Tanaka: Discover and Afterward." *Geijutsu Seikatsu*, May 1977. This article describes in detail Yasushi Tanaka's childhood and early school days in Japan. A monthly arts magazine, translated into English as "The Artistic Life," was published in Japan in the 1960s and 1970s and is out of print.
- Szabo, George, "Yasushi Tanaka 1886 - 1941, A Biography." Possibly an exhibition catalog of the Robert Lehman Collection, The Metropolitan Museum of Art, New York.
- Cann, Louise G., "For Art and Nature." Reprint of a lecture given on February 16, 1936, probably to the American Women's Club of Paris. Text reproduced in Japanese translation only on p. 69 of 1920-30's Rhapsody in Paris.

Don't miss out!

Visit the website below and you can sign up to receive emails whenever Denise Tanaka publishes a new book. There's no charge and no obligation.

https://books2read.com/r/B-A-UPKD-YBLUB

BOOKS 2 READ

Connecting independent readers to independent writers.

Also by Denise Tanaka

Wish and A Star
Truth in Cinders
Lady in White
INTANGIBLE: Yasushi Tanaka and Louise G. Cann, A Marriage of Artist and Author
Who Murdered Lizzie? My Family Story of the Brutal Crime of 1884 that Shocked the City of Roanoke, Virginia
Flowers for Dana: the 1949 Murder of Dana Marie Weaver in the "Star City" Roanoke, Virginia

Watch for more at sasorizabooks.com.

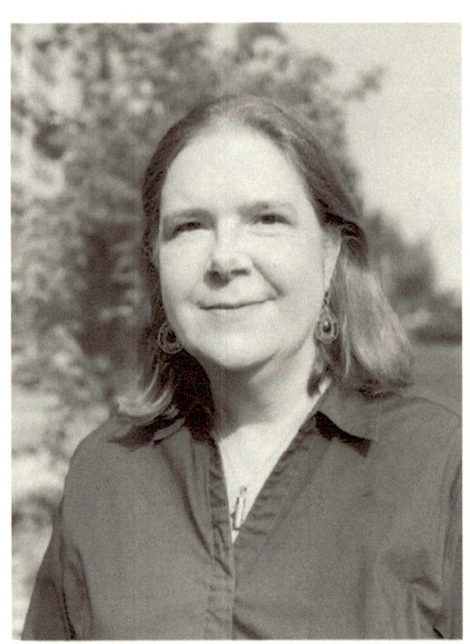

About the Author

Denise B. Tanaka has a lifelong passion for writing stories of magical beings and faraway worlds but is sometimes sidetracked by nonfiction projects. A graduate of Sonoma State University, she works as a senior paralegal in immigration law. She has dabbled in genealogy for more than 30 years and is very grateful for the internet.

Read more at sasorizabooks.com.

www.ingramcontent.com/pod-product-compliance
Lightning Source LLC
LaVergne TN
LVHW091005080826
845145LV00003B/1134

9781946055071